Communications
in Computer and Information Science   **408**

For further volumes:
http://www.springer.com/series/7899

Tristan Cazenave · Mark H.M. Winands
Hiroyuki Iida (Eds.)

Computer Games

Workshop on Computer Games, CGW 2013
Held in Conjunction with the 23rd International
Conference on Artificial Intelligence, IJCAI 2013
Beijing, China, August 3, 2013
Revised Selected Papers

Springer

Editors
Tristan Cazenave
Université Paris-Dauphine
Paris
France

Mark H.M. Winands
Universiteit Maastricht
Maastricht
The Netherlands

Hiroyuki Iida
School of Information Science
JAIST
Nomi
Japan

ISSN 1865-0929   ISSN 1865-0937 (electronic)
ISBN 978-3-319-05427-8   ISBN 978-3-319-05428-5 (eBook)
DOI 10.1007/978-3-319-05428-5
Springer Cham Heidelberg New York Dordrecht London

Library of Congress Control Number: 2014934688

Printed on acid-free paper

Springer is part of Springer Science+Business Media (www.springer.com)

Preface

These proceedings contain the papers of the Computer Games Workshop at IJCAI 2013 (CGW 2013) held in Beijing, China. The workshop took place August 3, 2013, in conjunction with the 23rd International Conference on Artificial Intelligence (IJCAI 2013). The Program Committee received 15 submissions. Each paper was sent to two referees. In the end, ten papers were accepted for presentation at the workshop, of which nine made it into these proceedings.

The published papers cover a wide range of topics related to computer games. They discuss six games that are played by humans in practice: Chess, Domineering, Chinese Checkers, Go, Goofspiel, and Tzaar. Moreover, there is one puzzle, the Sliding Tile Puzzle, one application, Cooperative Path-Finding problems, and one paper on General Game Playing. Below we provide a brief outline of the contributions, in the order in which they appear in the book.

"Monte-Carlo Fork Search for Cooperative Path-Finding" is authored by Bruno Bouzy. He proposes a new algorithm, called Monte-Carlo Fork Search (MCFS), which solves Cooperative Path-Finding (CPF) problems with simultaneity. Its background is Monte-Carlo Tree Search (MCTS) and Nested Monte-Carlo Search (NMCS). The key idea of MCFS is to build a search tree balanced over the whole game tree. After a simulation, MCFS stores the whole sequence of actions in the tree, which enables MCFS to fork new sequences at any depth in the built tree. The algorithm is suited for CPF problems in which the branching factor is too large for MCTS or A*, and in which congestion may arise at any distance from the initial state. With sufficient time and memory, Nested MCFS (NMCFS) solves congestion problems in the literature finding better solutions than the state-of-the-art solutions. It also solves N-puzzles without hole near-optimally.

"Building Large Compressed PDBs for the Sliding Tile Puzzle," written by Robert Döbbelin, Thorsten Schütt, and Alexander Reinefeld, describes the computation of 9-9-6, 9-8-7, and 8-8-8 Pattern Databases (PDB) for the 24-puzzle that are three orders of magnitude larger (up to 1.4 TB) than the 6-6-6-6 PDB. This is possible by performing a parallel breadth-first search in the compressed pattern space. Their experiments indicate an average eight-fold improvement of the 9-9-6 PDB over the 6-6-6-6 PDB for the 24-puzzle.

"Monte Carlo Tree Search in Simultaneous Move Games with Applications to Goofspiel" is a joint effort by Marc Lanctot, Viliam Lisý, and Mark Winands, and discusses the adaptation of MCTS to simultaneous move games with and without chance events. They introduced a new algorithm, Online Outcome Sampling (OOS), which approaches a Nash equilibrium strategy over time. The authors compare both head-to-head performance and exploitability of several MCTS variants in Goofspiel. The result reveals that regret matching and OOS performs best and that all variants produced less exploitable strategies than UCT.

"Decision Trees for Computer Go Features," by Francois van Niekerk and Steve Kroon, investigates the feasibility of using decision trees to generate features for guiding MCTS in Computer Go. Their approach employs queries that refine knowledge of the current board position as the tree is descended. The experiments show that while this approach exhibits potential, the initial prototype is not as powerful as using traditional pattern features.

"UCT Enhancements in Chinese Checkers Using an Endgame Database," is a contribution of Max Roschke and Nathan Sturtevant. They assessed the performance of MCTS-based AIs and the effectiveness of augmenting them with a lookup table containing evaluations of games states in the game of Chinese Checkers. The lookup table is only guaranteed to be correct during the endgame, but serves as an accurate heuristic throughout the game. Experiments show that using the lookup table only for its endgames is harmful, while using it for its heuristic values improves the quality of play. The research is performed on a board with 81 locations and 6 pieces, which is larger than previous work on lookup tables in Chinese Checkers. It is a precursor to using the 500-GB full-game single-agent data on the full-size board with 81 locations and 10 pieces.

"Automated Generation of New Concepts from General Game Playing," by Yuichiro Sato and Tristan Cazenave, describes how to extract explicit concepts from heuristic functions obtained using a simulation-based approach. The proposed algorithm quickly learns new concepts without any supervision but from experience in the environment. Concepts to understand the semantics of Tic-tac-toe are generated by their approach. These concepts are also available to understand the semantics of Connect Four. The authors conclude that their approach is applicable to General Game Playing and is able to extract explicit concepts, which are able to be understood by humans.

"WALTZ: A Strong Tzaar-Playing Program," written by Tomáš Valla and Pavel Veselý, introduces the game of Tzaar, part of the Project GIPF, to the AI community. It is an abstract strategy two-player game, which has recently gained popularity in the gaming community and has won several awards. The high branching factor makes Tzaar a difficult game for computers. The authors present WALTZ, a strong Tzaar-playing program, using enhanced variants of $\alpha\beta$ and proof-number search. After many tests with computer opponents and a year of deployment on a popular board-gaming portal, the authors conclude that WALTZ can defeat all available computer programs and even strong human players.

"Perfectly Solving Domineering Boards," by Jos Uiterwijk, presents the author's research in the game of Domineering. For this game the author defined 12 knowledge rules, of increasing complexity. Of these rules, six can be used to show that the starting player (assumed to be Vertical) can win a game against any opposition, while six can be used to prove a definite loss (a win for the second player, Horizontal). Applying this knowledge-based method to all 81 rectangular boards up to 10×10 (omitting the trivial $1 \times n$ and $m \times 1$ boards), 67 could be solved perfectly. This is in sharp contrast with previous publications reporting the solution of Domineering boards, where only a few tiny boards were solved perfectly, the remainder requiring up to large amounts of search. Applying this method to larger boards with one or both sizes up to 30 solves 216 more boards, mainly with one dimension odd. All results fully agree with previously reported game-theoretic values.

"How Relevant Are Chess Composition Conventions?" is a contribution by Azlan Iqbal. Using an existing experimentally validated computational aesthetics model for three-move mate problems, the author analyzes sets of computer-generated chess compositions adhering to at least two, three and four comparable conventions to test whether simply conforming to more conventions has a positive effect on their aesthetics, as is generally believed by human composers. The paper also analyzes human judge scores of 145 three-move mate problems composed by humans to see if they have any positive correlation with the computational aesthetic scores of those problems. The results suggest two main things. First, the right amount of adherence to composition conventions in a composition has a positive effect on its perceived aesthetics. Second, human judges either do not look at the same conventions related to aesthetics in the model used or emphasize others that have less to do with beauty as perceived by the majority of players, even though they may mistakenly consider their judgments "beautiful" in the traditional, non-esoteric sense.

This book would not have been produced without the help of many persons. In particular, we would like to mention the authors and referees for their help. Moreover, the organizers of IJCAI 2013 contributed substantially by bringing the researchers together.

December 2013

Tristan Cazenave
Mark H.M. Winands
Hiroyuki Iida

Organization

Program Committee Chairs

Tristan Cazenave	Université Paris-Dauphine, France
Hiroyuki Iida	JAIST, Japan
Mark H.M. Winands	Maastricht University, The Netherlands

Program Committee

Yngvi Björnsson	CADIA, Reykjavik University, Iceland
Bruno Bouzy	Université Paris-Descartes, France
Michael Buro	University of Alberta, Canada
Tristan Cazenave	Université Paris-Dauphine, France
Remi Coulom	Université Lille 3, France
Stefan Edelkamp	University of Bremen, Germany
Hiroyuki Iida	JAIST, Japan
Eric Jacopin	CREC Saint-Cyr, France
Nicolas Jouandeau	Université Paris 8, France
Sylvain Lagrue	Université de Lens, France
Marc Lanctot	Maastricht University, The Netherlands
Jean Méhat	Université Paris 8, France
Martin Müller	University of Alberta, Canada
Abdallah Saffidine	Université Paris-Dauphine, France
Maarten Schadd	Maastricht University, The Netherlands
Nathan Sturtevant	University of Denver, USA
Fabien Teytaud	Université du Littoral, France
Olivier Teytaud	Université Paris-Sud, France
Mark H.M. Winands	Maastricht University, The Netherlands
I-Chen Wu	National Chiao-Tung University, Taiwan

Contents

Monte-Carlo Fork Search for Cooperative Path-Finding 1
  Bruno Bouzy

Building Large Compressed PDBs for the Sliding Tile Puzzle 16
  Robert Döbbelin, Thorsten Schütt, and Alexander Reinefeld

Monte Carlo Tree Search in Simultaneous Move Games
with Applications to Goofspiel 28
  Marc Lanctot, Viliam Lisý, and Mark H.M. Winands

Decision Trees for Computer Go Features 44
  Francois van Niekerk and Steve Kroon

UCT Enhancements in Chinese Checkers Using an Endgame Database 57
  Max Roschke and Nathan R. Sturtevant

Automated Generation of New Concepts from General Game Playing 71
  Yuichiro Sato and Tristan Cazenave

WALTZ: A Strong Tzaar-Playing Program 81
  Tomáš Valla and Pavel Veselý

Perfectly Solving Domineering Boards 97
  Jos W.H.M. Uiterwijk

How Relevant Are Chess Composition Conventions? 122
  Azlan Iqbal

Author Index 133

Monte-Carlo Fork Search for Cooperative Path-Finding

Bruno Bouzy(✉)

LIPADE, Université Paris Descartes, Paris, France
bruno.bouzy@parisdescartes.fr

Abstract. This paper presents Monte-Carlo Fork Search (MCFS), a new algorithm that solves Cooperative Path-Finding (CPF) problems with simultaneity. The background is Monte-Carlo Tree Search (MCTS) and Nested Monte-Carlo Search (NMCS). Concerning CPF, MCFS avoids to enter into the curse of the very high branching factor. Regarding MCTS, the key idea of MCFS is to build a tree balanced over the whole game tree. To do so, after a simulation, MCFS stores the whole sequence of actions in the tree, which enables MCFS to fork new sequences at any depth in the built tree. This idea fits CPF problems in which the branching factor is too large for MCTS or A* approaches, and in which congestion may arise at any distance from the start state. With sufficient time and memory, Nested MCFS (NMCFS) solves congestion problems in the literature finding better solutions than the state-of-the-art solutions, and it solves N-puzzles without hole near-optimally. The algorithm is anytime and complete. The scalability of the approach is shown for gridsize up to 200×200 and up to 400 agents.

1 Introduction

Cooperative pathfinding (CPF) addresses the problem of finding paths for a set of agents, for them to move to their goals. At each timestep, every agent moves to a neighbouring cell. The set of agents has to find the minimal cost for reaching its set of goals. The cost is the elapsed time. There are two families of approaches: the coupled approach and the decoupled approach. In the coupled approach, the whole set of agents is considered as one. One main bottleneck is the size of the set of joint actions which is exponential in the number of agents. In the decoupled approach, each agent is considered individually and the main obstacle is managing the collisions between the agents.

A* is the prototype of the coupled approach. A* with operator decomposition (A*+OD) [16] is a speed-up version of A*. ICTS [14] searches a solution in an Incremental Cost Tree (ICT). The weakness of the coupled approach is its inability to solve large problems or including complex coordination between agents. However, very recently, a new work, TOMPP [21], modeling multi-agent pathfinding as a network flow, contradicts this statement. Windowed Hierarchical Cooperative A* (WHCA*) [15] illustrates the decoupled approach.

T. Cazenave et al. (Eds.): CGW 2013, CCIS 408, pp. 1–15, 2014.
DOI: 10.1007/978-3-319-05428-5_1, © Springer International Publishing Switzerland 2014

Push&Swap (P&S) [9] solves CPF problems on graphs with at least 2 empty cells. TASS (Tree-based Agent Swapping Strategy) is designed to solve problems with at most 4 empty cells [5,6]. These solvers are very fast but they cannot improve their solution with more computing time.

In this paper we present Monte-Carlo Fork Search (MCFS) and its nested version Nested Monte-Carlo Fork Search (NMCFS) for CPF. The background is Monte-Carlo Tree Search (MCTS) [7] and NMCS [3]. MCTS and NMCS have been applied with success to many planning problems such as Morpion Solitaire [12]. However, their weakness lies in their inability to deal with the high branching factor of CPF problems. To solve CPF problems, our goal is to design a new algorithm that has the strength of MCTS and NMCS, and is not sensitive to the branching factor. The key idea is to make the built tree cover all the interesting parts of the game tree in a balanced way.

Like MCTS, MCFS is anytime. It has been compared to TOMPP, TASS, and Push&Swap on their test problems: specific congestion problems [5,8], and N-puzzles without hole problems with simultaneous actions [21]. For scalability, MCFS has been assessed on grids with size up to 200×200, with obstacles (20 %) and with a number of agents up to 400. Some of the results obtained with the parallel criterion are manually proved optimal, and the others are conjectured to be near-optimal. The results are translated into the sequential criterion to be compared with the numerous work using this criterion, and we show that MCFS obtains better results on this criterion.

The outline of the paper is the following. First, we give the CPF problem definition. Secondly, we relate previous work on CPF and on MCTS. Thirdly, we present the MCFS and NMCFS algorithms. Fourthly, we describe the experiments and the significant results. Fifthly, we discuss the properties of the algorithm. Finally, we conclude and present future work.

2 CPF Problem Definition

The CPF literature contains a lot of work. Each work uses its specific criteria to define the problem, which makes comparisons difficult. In the literature, the cells are mostly squares used with 4-connectivity or 8-connectivity. Whatever the grid connectivity, an agent can move on the neighbouring cells or stay, and respect the two following rules: No two agents can be on the same cell (**Rule 0**), No two agents can swap (**Rule 1**). With 8-connectivity, specialized rules must define whether two agents may cross diagonally or not, whether an agent can move diagonally when one obstacle is on its side, or whether it can cross two obstacles situated on a diagonal. In this paper, we use squares and 4-connectivity with rule 0 and rule 1 only.

The most important feature is the simultaneity or sequentiality of elementary actions. A lot of work fall in the sequential category. In this work, we use simultaneous, parallel moves. When the elementary actions are executed in parallel, the agents must respect rule 0: when several agents wish to move towards the same cell, only one of them can actually move to the cell. However, an agent may

Table 1. A simple CPF problem (problem 520 of [6]). In a cell, the first symbol represents either an obstacle (x), or void (_) or the number of the agent occupying the cell. When present, the second number represents the number of the agent whose goal is to reach this cell. For instance, agent number 1 is occupying the lower right cell. Its goal is to reach the cell situated on the second row and the second column.

```
2 _    x x    4 _    x x
_ 3    _ 1    _ 2    x x
3 _    x x    _ 4    1 _
```

Table 2. A solution to the CPF problem of Table 1. The movements of the agents are shown in bold. The number of timesteps equals 6. The sum of elementary actions equals 17. This solution is TIME and SUM optimal.

```
 _ _ |x x|_ _ |x x     _ _ |x x|_ _ |x x     _ _ |x x|1 _|x x
 2 3 |_ 1|4 2|x x      2 3 |4 1|1 2|x x      3 3 |2 1|4 2|x x
 3 _ |x x|1 4|_ _      3 _ |x x|_ 4|_ _      _ _ |x x|_ 4|_ _
        t = 1                  t = 2                  t = 3

 _ _ |x x|1 _|x x      _ _ |x x|_ _ |x x     _ _ |x x|_ _ |x x
 3 3 |_ 1|2 2|x x      3 3 |_ 1|1 2|x x      3 3 |1 1|2 2|x x
 _ _ |x x|4 4|_ _      _ _ |x x|2 4|4 _      _ _ |x x|4 4|_ _
        t = 4                  t = 5                  t = 6
```

move to an occupied cell provided that this cell is freed by its occupant during the timestep. Therefore, it is worth noting than joint actions including circular elementary actions are possible. For instance, 4 agents situated on 4 adjacent cells can move circularly.

In the multi-agent context, two targets can be optimized: the sum of individual costs (**SUM**), the number of timesteps (**TIME**). In most work [6,9,14–16], the optimized target is SUM. However, in this paper, we optimize TIME, that is to say the global elapsed time. Some work such as [21] fall into this category. The number of timesteps is also commonly called makespan. Comparing work optimizing SUM with our work is still possible provided that we estimate the SUM target by counting the elementary actions of the sequences found.

At each timestep, an agent can either stay on its cell or move to an adjacent cell provided it respects rule 0 and rule 1. During a timestep, all the agents act simultaneously. The joint goal is found when all the agents have reached their individual goals. The problem is to find the minimum number of timesteps to reach the joint goal. Table 1 shows an instance of a CPF problem on a 3 × 4 grid. Table 2 shows an optimal solution to this problem. In the following, a position refers to the set of positions of the agents. A path, a plan, an episode, a simulation refer to the same concept: a sequence of positions linked two-by-two by a joint action. The goal is the final position. A hole is an empty cell. A CPF problem may have or not have holes.

3 Related Work

This section presents related work on CPF, and related work on MCTS.

3.1 Cooperative Path-Finding

The starting point of CPF is centralized A*. A* works optimally on very small problems with very few agents. To avoid the exponential number of actions in the number of agents, Standley has proposed Operator Decomposition (OD) [16]. A*+OD and an admissible heuristic are optimal [16].

ICTS [14] is a two-level search: a global level and a low level. At the global level, the search proceeds on an Incremental Cost Tree (ICT) in which one node corresponds to a vector of costs. At depth δ, the sum of the costs of a node is the optimal cost plus δ. A node is a goal for ICT when there is an effective combination of individual paths without conflict and with costs corresponding to the costs of the node.

TOMPP [20,21] optimizes the global elapsed time. It models a multi-agent path-finding problem as a network flow and shows the equivalence between the two models. It uses integer linear programming to solve the network flow problem and the multi-agent path-finding problem as a consequence. TOMPP is tested on the N-puzzle without hole, and in many-agents-many-obstacles problems. TOMPP is time-optimal.

In video games, the optimal methods are not used because they are not scalable. Adaptations of A* are used instead. Windowed HCA* (WHCA*) decomposes the whole task into a series of single agent searches and searches m-steps plans [15]. Sub-optimal methods with some completeness guarantees on well-specified sub-classes of problems give good results: P&S [9] solves CPF problems on graphs with at least 2 empty cells. TASS (Tree-based Agent Swapping Strategy) [6] is designed to solve problems with at most 4 empty cells. Reference [5,8] provide interesting test problems. MAPP (Multi-Agent Path Planning) [19] defines the Slideable class and presents a method complete on this class of problems.

3.2 MCTS

MCTS is the approach that revolutionized computer go in 2006 with the UCT method [7] and the Go playing programs Crazy Stone [4] or MoGo [13]. In the following years, MCTS was also successful in many other games and planning problems [2]. MCTS iteratively expands a tree starting a the root, and launches simulations to obtain rewards at the end of the games. An iteration has four phases: selection, expansion, simulation and propagation. In the selection phase, MCTS starts at the root of the tree and go down to a leaf node by using the UCB rule [1]. When reaching a node not fully expanded, MCTS chooses the next state with its simulation policy, and adds the corresponding node into the tree. Then MCTS starts the simulation phase. At the end of the simulation, the reward is obtained and propagated into the nodes browsed by the selection phase.

4 MCFS

First, this section presents the rationale of MCFS. Secondly, since MCFS is largely inspired from MCTS, this section shows the similarities and the differences with MCTS. Thirdly, it presents the algorithm in its nested version (NMCFS) or not (MCFS). Fourthly, it describes how the basic simulations are performed, and fifthly, it presents the necessary pre and post-processing. The guidelines of MCFS are:

- not entering into the curse of the branching factor,
- making use of the whole simulation to build the tree,
- forking new paths at appropriate nodes of the built tree.

First, the branching factor of CPF problems being very high, the move generation itself can be problematic (see for instance N-puzzles without hole) and very time consuming when complete.

Secondly, after performing a simulation, nothing forbids to store the whole simulation to use it later.

Thirdly, a previous simulation being given, a natural idea is to improve this simulation by forking a new one starting at a promising node of this sequence.

4.1 Similarities and Differences with MCTS

Like MCTS, MCFS iteratively builds a tree with four stages: selection, expansion, simulation and propagation. The simulation stage and the propagation stage in MCFS remain identical to the corresponding stages in MCTS. Like MCTS, MCFS uses the optimism faced to uncertainty principle by using the UCB rule [1]. The difference between MCTS and MCFS mainly lies in the manner the game tree is explored, in the manner the start of the next simulation is selected, and in the manner the built tree is expanded at each iteration. MCTS explores the game tree by respecting a width principle: at a node, MCTS prefers to explore an unexplored action rather than an already explored child node. Consequently, MCTS can be stuck near the root if the branching factor is high. The tree built by MCTS browses the upper part of the game tree only. Moreover, the next simulation starts from a leaf node of the built tree. Furthermore, in standard MCTS, MCTS adds one node after each simulation.

MCFS explores the game tree in a depth-first manner. First, after each iteration, *all* the states encountered during the simulation become nodes added into the MCFS tree. Secondly, at the beginning of an iteration, with the help of the UCB rule, MCFS selects the best node to fork, among *all* the nodes of the built tree. This is very different from the MCTS selection stage that starts from the root node and iteratively chooses a child node with the UCB rule until it reaches a node with an unexplored action. In MCFS, the next simulation starts from this selected node which is an interior node of the built tree. In MCFS, the built tree has only one leaf node: the goal node.

Figure 1 shows an overview of how the trees built by MCFS and MCTS fill the whole game tree. As iterations are going on, the MCTS tree is deepening, and the

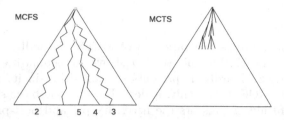

Fig. 1. The tree built by MCFS (left) and MCTS (right) within the game tree represented by a triangle. The root is at the top. The goal is the bottom line. Each action is a small straight line. The circles represent nodes whith a fork. The numbers are the iteration numbers.

MCFS tree is widening. At iteration 1, a length-12 sequence is found. The second iteration selects the root as a starting node, and a length-15 sequence is found. Iteration 3 selects a node situated at depth 2 on the current best sequence, and finds a length-15 sub-sequence giving a length-17 sequence. Iteration 4 selects a node at depth 4 and finds a sub-sequence of length 5 giving a length-9 sequence, the new current best. Iteration 5, selects a node at depth 6 and finds a sub-sequence of length 2 giving a sequence of length 8, the new current best. And so on until the iteration budget is exhausted. The idea to allow MCFS to fork sub-sequences anywhere in the game tree is respected.

4.2   MCFS and NMCFS Algorithms

Since the pseudo-code of NMCFS is very similar to that of MCFS, Algorithm 1 directly shows the pseudo-code for NMCFS. (The MCFS pseudo-code corresponds to the NMCFS pseudo-code with $lev = 1$). NMCFS takes the starting position (a), the goal position (b) and the nesting level (lev) as inputs. NMCFS returns the length of the best plan found ($bestSeq$) (line 1). If the level is zero, NMCFS calls *sample* the basic simulation function. n is the number of simulations performed so far. $lmin$ contains the current best length. $actualSeq$ is the sequence of positions played at each iteration. $root$ is the root node initialized with the starting position a. NMCFS is a while loop (lines 7–14). it is the number of iterations to perform. During an iteration, the best node of the tree is selected (line 8) with Eq. 1. NMCFS is called, starting on this node with the nesting level minus one (line 9). The length of the simulation plus the depth of the node in the tree is compared to $lmin$ (line 10). If the comparaison holds, $lmin$ and $bestSeq$ are updated (line 11). The nodes between the selected node and the root are updated with l, and the tree is expanded by adding $actualSeq$ to it (*backUp* and *append* line 13).

In Eq. 1, it is essential to notice that $argmin$ is applied *over the whole tree*, whis is very different from the MCTS selection. $nd.lmin + nd.depth$ is used as an exploitation term to focus the search near the current best sequence. Concerning the exploration term, C is a parameter set experimentally. *var* is the variance

```
1  int NMCFS(a, b, bestSeq, lev)
2  begin
3     if lev == 0 then
4        return sample(a, b, actualSeq)
5     end
6     n = 1 ; lmin = +∞ ; actualSeq ; Node root(a)
7     while n ≤ it do
8        Node nd = root.selectNode() ; pos = nd.positions
9        l = NMCFS(pos, b, actualSeq, lev − 1)
10       if l + nd.depth < lmin then
11          lmin = l + nd.depth ; bestSeq = seq(root(a), nd) + actualSeq
12       end
13       nd.backUp(l) ; nd.append(actualSeq, l, b) ; n = n + 1
14    end
15    return lmin
16 end
```

Algorithm 1: NMCFS

over the lengths of the sequences going through the node. It enables MCFS to prefer nodes with high variance. $nForks$ is the number of times the node has been selected so far. $log(n)$ makes it possible to forget no node for n sufficiently large.

$$nd = \arg\min_{builttree}(lmin + depth − C\sqrt{\frac{var \log(n)}{1 + nForks}}) \qquad (1)$$

4.3   Basic Simulations

Algorithm 2 shows function $sample$ that executes a basic simulation starting on position p. seq contains the actual sequence played out. l is the current length of the simulation. It executes a loop while the goal is not reached and l does not exceed ls the maximal length of sequences. The joint action is determined by $pseudoRandomChoice$. It returns a joint action according to a pseudo-random policy. $pseudoRandomChoice$ does not enumerate all the joint actions, which could be tricky when the number of agents is large. Instead, each agent says which cell it wants to move on: its wish. If all the wishes are compatible with Rule 0 and Rule 1, then the joint action is valid and returned. When two wishes are in conflict, the conflict is solved by prioritizing one agent over the other at random. When all the conflicts are solved, the wishes become the actual elementary actions, and the joint action is returned. If some conflicts cannot be solved after a given number of tries, then the agents relax their wish, and the wishes are formulated again. Without relaxing the wishes, the joint action contains optimal elementary actions only. With relaxing, the joint action may also contain non optimal elementary actions. The function $play$ transforms the position according to the effects of the joint action.

```
1 int sample(p, b, seq) begin
2     l = 0
3     while ((p ≠ b) and (l < ls)) do
4         action = pseudoRandomChoice(b)
5         p = play(p, action) ; seq[l] = p ; l = l + 1
6     end
7     return l
8 end
```

Algorithm 2: Sample

4.4   Pre and Post Processing

Before launching NMCFS, all the distances between two cells assuming the obstacles and no agent are computed, and stored in a table to be used in the simulations. After completing a best simulation, NMCFS counts the number of elementary actions used.

5   Experiments

This section describes the test set, the experimental settings and the results.

5.1   Set of Problems

To assess our approach, we have taken three kinds of problems. First, we addressed the congestion problems of TASS and Push&Swap. Reference [5] contains six interesting problems which we named from 515 up to 520. Problem 5xy refers to the problem defined by figure 5.xy pages 58–61 in [5]. For instance, 515 contains 10 agents with 19 cells and 520 contains 4 agents with 8 cells (see Table 1). Reference [9] contains eight specific problems: Tree, Corners, Tunnel, String, Loopchain, Connector, Rotation, and Stacks. The first six problems contain between 3 and 7 agents on small graphs with at most 18 nodes. The last two problems have 16 agents with 24 or 25 nodes.

Secondly, we addressed some N-puzzle problems with one hole ($N = 8$, 15, 24) or no hole ($N = 9$, 16, 25). The N-puzzle problem with one hole in which SUM is optimized is known to be NP-hard [11]. The N-puzzle problem without hole in which TIME is optimized is very representative of the CPF class of problems.

Thirdly, we addressed medium-sized-to-large-grid-many-agents-with-obstacles problems with a low level of congestion. References [16, 17] contain two such examples which we call $s10$ and $s11$. In video games, the problems encountered may have one thousand agents or more [19]. Furthermore, they may have large grids, like 512×512 in reference benchmarks [18]. However, we have generated smaller problems: random problems on 25×25 grids, with 125 (20 %) obstacles and 100 agents, on 100×100 grids with 400 agents and 2000 (20 %) obstacles, and on 200×200 grids with 400 agents and 4000 (10 %) obstacles.

5.2   Experimental Settings

The experiments were performed with elementary actions played simultaneously, with 4-connectivity, and TIME as target of optimization. *maxpl* is the heuristic value using the maximum over the individual path lengths. $C = 1$. $ls = 500$. For each problem and each algorithm, we give the number of time steps used (*nts*) and the number of elementary actions used (*nea*) to solve the problem. Furthermore, we mention the computing time spent, the nesting level (*lv*) and the number of iterations for each level (*il*). We used a 3.2 Ghz computer with 6 Gb to perform the experiments. We compare the results of NMCFS to those of TASS [5], Push&Swap [8,9] and TOMPP [21].

Two points must be specified to reproduce the experiments and obtain the same results. First, because a CPF problem is reversible, bi-directional search [10] is suited to CPF problems, and the results shown in the paper were actually obtained with a bi-directional NMCFS. However, this point, subject of another work, is not presented here, not to obscure the presentation of NMCFS. Secondly, we obtained the results with a version of NMCFS slightly different from Algorithm 1: line 4 was replaced by a call to an adapted level-1 MC search [3] in which the branching factor was limited by $2 + maxpl$. And the adapted level-1 MC search calls the *sample* function of Algorithm 2. This means that the actual number of levels used by a search is $lev + 1$ actually: the number of levels used by Algorithm 1 plus one used by the adapted level-1 MC search. The *lev* variable in the tables correspond to *lev* in Algorithm 1.

5.3   Results

This section presents the results obtained by NMCFS on congestion problems, on N-puzzle problems and on many-agent-large-grid problems.

Congestion Problems. Table 3 shows the results on Khorshid's congestion problems. For each problem, the table gives *nea* of TASS, *nea* and *nts* of NMCFS and *Optim*. In order to underline the anytime property of NMCFS, the table gives *nts* and *nea* obtained by NMCFS for relevant time constraints. For a time t, the number of levels (*lev*) and the number of iterations per level (*il*) are provided as well. The results in terms of *nts* are new. For the first four problems, we found the optimal value (*Optim*) with paper and pen, and NMCFS found the optimal values for these problems. For problems 516 and 515, we do not know if the solutions are optimal or not. In terms of *nea*, and without considering the time constraint, NMCFS outperforms TASS. The harder the problem, the larger the difference. However, TASS solves all the problems in less than one second. NMCFS solved the easy problems in less than one second, but used three days for problem 516 to find out the last value in the table. With less than 3 days of time, NMCFS was not able to solve the problems of [5] which are more complex than problems 515 and 516. Finally, the table shows that, in one second of time, NMCFS finds out better *nea* values than TASS on problems 520, 519, 518, 517

Table 3. Results on Khorshid's congestion problems.

	TASS	NMCFS					Optim	
	nea	t	nts	nea	lev	il	nts	nea
520	34	0.1s	6	17	2	5	6	17
519	30	0.03s	8	18	2	5	8	12
518	58	1s	15	40	1	5	10	≤ 26
		10s	11	34	2	14		
		1m	10	32	2	40		
517	170	1s	31	105	1	4	13	≤ 31
		10s	17	67	2	7		
		1m	13	51	2	18		
		3m	13	31	2	30		
515	459	1s	34	159	1	3	≤ 15	≤ 71
		10s	26	133	1	36		
		1m	19	111	1	256		
		10m	17	103	2	60		
		30m	15	71	3	40		
516	234	1m	167	464	1	2	≤ 19	≤ 78
		10m	63	250	1	20		
		1h	45	216	2	10		
		10h	27	128	2	40		
		3 days	19	78	3	30		

and 515. NMCFS needs one hour to find a better solution than TASS on problem 516.

Table 4 shows the results on Luna's congestion problems. For each relevant time constraint, this table gives the same kind of information as Table 3. Again, the results in terms of nts are new. For the problems Rotation, Tree, String, Corners and Loopchain, we found the *Optim* value with paper and pen. NMCFS found the optimal value for Rotation, Tree, String, and Corners but not for Loopchain. For Tunnel and Connector, we do not know if the results are optimal or not. In terms of nea, and without considering the time constraint, NMCFS outperforms Push&Swap. For Loopchain, the difference is large. Push&Swap solves all the problems in a few seconds [9]. NMCFS solves the easy problems in less than one second, but used several hours for Loopchain. The table shows that, in one second of time, NMCFS finds out better nea values than Push&Swap on problems Rotation, Tree, String, and Corners. But NMCFS needs one minute to find a better solution than Push&Swap on problem Connection, few minutes on problem Tunnel, and ten seconds for problem Loopchain.

N-puzzle Problems. Table 5 shows the results obtained by NMCFS on puzzle problems. For the 8-Puzzle, NMCFS found the optimal solution quickly. For the 5×5-puzzle, NMCFS is slightly sub-optimal because the optimal length is 7 [20], and NMCFS found a solution of length 8. Table 6 gives the best solution found by NMCFS on this problem. For the other puzzles, NMCFS found solutions for which the optimality remains unknown. For each problem, Table 5 also gives the branching factor to show that NMCFS is not constrained by this feature.

Table 4. Results on Luna's congestion problems.

	Push&Swap	NMCFS					Optim	
	nea	t	nts	nea	lev	il	nts	nea
rotation	18	0.01s	1	16	1	1	1	16
tree	18	0.01s	6	12	1	5	6	12
string	26	0.02s	8	20	1	5	8	20
corners	50	1s	8	32	2	5	8	32
connection	86	1s	20	96	1	10	≤ 16	≤ 70
		10s	18	90	1	150		
		1m	16	70	2	20		
tunnel	81	1s	90	221	1	2	≤ 15	≤ 49
		10s	43	109	1	16		
		1m	34	95	1	96		
		10m	20	57	2	32		
		1h	15	49	3	30		
loopchain	350	10s	69	290	1	2	≤ 17	≤ 95
		1m	65	234	1	16		
		10m	48	176	1	160		
		1h	33	144	2	32		
		12h	19	95	3	200		

Table 5. Results and branching factors (bf) on N-puzzle problems.

nAgents	branchFactor	NMCFS				
		t	nts	nea	level	it.p.lev.
8	123	0.1s	4	26	1	10
9	27	1s	8	48	1	3
		5s	6	38	1	10
15	3815	1s	12	128	1	3
		10s	11	112	1	100
		1m	9	94	2	34
		10m	8	90	2	120
		20m	7	84	3	50
16	951	1s	14	128	1	1
		10s	13	128	1	10
		1m	10	106	1	100
		10m	10	106	2	35
		1h	8	96	3	80
24	$\approx 10^5$	1s	20	269	1	1
		10s	16	295	1	16
		1m	11	201	1	120
		10m	11	181	2	32
		1h	9	171	3	17
		10h	7	141	3	30
25	$\approx 3 \times 10^4$	10s	27	400	1	1
		1m	21	258	1	10
		10m	16	218	2	11
		1h	13	218	2	25
		10h	9	152	2	90
		30h	8	120	3	30

Many-Agents-Large-Grid Problems. Table 7 shows the results achieved by NMCFS on large grids with many agents. na is the number of agents, $nobs$ the number of obstacles, pb the problem, and h the $maxpl$ value.

On 25×25 gridsize problems with 20 % of obstacles and 100 agents, we performed two experiments. One experiment shows the result obtained with one simulation at level 1. One simulation lasts about 1 minute on average. In this setting, nea ranges in the interval 2480, 2825 with 2650 on average. A second

Table 6. From left to right, the best sequence found on the 5 × 5-puzzle problem without hole [20] ($nts = 8$ and $nea = 120$). The elementary moves are in bold type style.

13	17	4	14	23	**1**	**13**	9	**4**	**14**	1	13	9	4	14
1	22	9	12	7	**11**	**17**	**15**	**12**	**23**	11	17	6	**15**	**12**
11	16	15	8	21	**16**	**22**	6	**21**	7	16	22	5	21	23
25	24	6	19	20	**24**	3	5	8	**19**	24	3	**2**	8	**7**
10	3	5	2	18	**25**	**10**	2	**18**	**20**	25	10	**18**	**20**	**19**
	$t = 0$					$t = 1$					$t = 2$			
1	13	9	4	14	**11**	**1**	**13**	9	4	1	**3**	13	9	4
11	17	6	15	12	**17**	3	6	15	14	11	**6**	**2**	**5**	15
22	3	**2**	**5**	23	22	**10**	2	**5**	**12**	**17**	**8**	**10**	**12**	**14**
16	**10**	**8**	**21**	7	16	**8**	**21**	7	23	**22**	**21**	7	**23**	19
24	**25**	18	20	19	24	25	18	20	19	16	**24**	**25**	18	20
	$t = 3$					$t = 4$					$t = 5$			
1	3	13	9	**4**	1	**2**	**3**	9	4	1	2	3	4	**5**
6	**2**	**10**	5	**15**	**6**	**8**	**13**	**10**	**5**	6	7	8	**9**	**10**
11	**8**	7	**12**	**14**	11	**7**	**12**	**14**	**15**	11	**12**	**13**	14	15
17	**22**	**23**	**18**	19	**16**	**17**	**18**	**19**	**20**	16	17	18	19	20
16	**21**	**24**	**25**	20	**21**	**22**	**23**	**24**	**25**	21	22	23	24	25
	$t = 6$					$t = 7$					$t = 8$			

Table 7. Results on large grids with obstacles and many agents.

gridsize	na	nobs	pb	nts	h	nea	t	lv	il
8 × 8	11	15	10	12	12	63	0.1s	1	5
			11	11	11	48			
25 × 25	100	125	1	45	41	2480	30s	1	1
			2	49	43	2590	1m		
			3	56	41	2748	2m		
			4	53	40	2825	2m		
			1	43	41	2351	6h	2	50
			2	43	43	2508			
			3	44	41	2460			
			4	44	40	2569			
100 × 100	100	1000	1	164	164	6879	1m	1	1
	200	2000	1	165	165	14203	5m		
	400	2000	1	171	171	33286	15m		
200 × 200	400	4000	1	344	344	55620	1h		

experiment gives the values obtained in 6 hours at level 2 with 50 iterations. Here, nea ranges in the interval 2350, 2570 with 2470 on average. Our values can be compared with the values in the literature: for a 30 × 20 grid with 100 agents and 17 % of obstacles, [9] mentions the average solution quality for WHCA* and P&S of 2700 and 2300 respectively. This is to show that, in this set of problems, the values obtained in one iteration at level one are not bad already, and that they are not much enhanced by the level-2 search. Knowing how far from optimality is level-2 search remains a question.

Table 7 also shows the results achieved by NMCFS on 100 × 100 grids with up to 400 agents and 2000 obstacles. With such level of congestion (20 % of obstacles and 4 % of agents), NMCFS at level 2 finds "good" solutions - not to say near-optimal. On 200 × 200 grids with 400 agents and 4000 obstacles, since the congestion is very low (10 % of obstacles and 1 % of agents), NMCFS finds the optimal solution despite the size of the grid and the time spent to

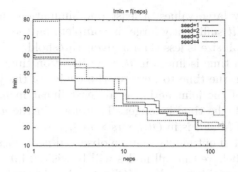

Fig. 2. *lmin* (i.e. *nts*) decreasing with the iteration number (*neps*) on four runs of MCFS on the loopchain problem at level 2.

perform it (one hour). To conclude this section, we see that the time to perform one simulation on large boards with many agents remains the limitation of the approach.

6   Discussion

This section discusses some properties of MCFS: the anytime property, memory use, completeness, optimality and computation time. Let it be the number of iterations, na the number of agents, gs the gridsize, ls the length of the simulations, nlv the number of nesting levels, and nnd the number of nodes.

The anytime property was detailed by the tables giving the results. $NMCFS$ obtains a first value after its first simulation, and progressively improves this value as time is going on. Figure 2 graphically illustrates the anytime property of MCFS.

Concerning memory use, most of the memory used by MCFS concerns nnd. nnd is linear in it, and linear in ls (which mainly depends on gs). The size of a node depends linearly on na. Memory used by MCFS is in $O(na \times it \times ls)$. Nesting MCFS permits to build smaller trees at each nesting level and to save memory. The memory used by NMCFS is in $O(na \times nlv \times it^{1/nlv} \times ls)$.

To discuss the completeness of the approach, we have to prove that at least one simulation will reach the goal. For the bad cases, MCFS uses pseudo-random simulations that are not biased: all the elementary actions are drawn with the uniform distribution of probability. The set of agents executes a random walk on a finite graph of the problem. All actions are reversible. The set of agents cannot be trapped in a dead-end. If a problem is solvable, there is a sequence linking the starting position to the goal, and given a sufficiently large number of timesteps, a random walk on this graph encounters the goal position. However, if the number of timesteps is finite, which is the case in practice, then some random walks do not encounter the goal. If the number of timesteps is large enough, a random walk reaches the goal with a probability $p > 0$. With a sufficiently large number of random walks, the goal will be reached at least once. Provided we set up ls

and *it* at sufficiently large values, a least one simulation succeeds. Therefore, MCFS, with *ls* and *it* sufficiently large, is complete on the set of solvable CPF problems whose graph size is less than a given threshold.

The computation time is linear in *it*. One iteration time is mainly linear in *ls*. At each timestep, the time to perform the choice of the joint action and to process the effects of the joint action is at least linear in *na*. When collisions have to be managed, the time is longer. Therefore, in the good case only, the computation time of MCFS is in $O(it \times ls \times na)$.

We have no proof of optimality, but we observed near-optimality in practice. Asymptotically, we believe that all nodes will be visited infinitely, and the best sequence found. The problem is that MCFS tackles the problem by lowering its current upper bound progressively without using any measure of near-optimality. The relevant question is which value of *it* garantees MCFS to find the optimal solution.

7   Conclusion

In this paper, we have described both MCFS, a new algorithm inspired from MCTS, that solves CPF problems, known for their very high branching factor, and NMCFS its nested version. MCFS works well on CPF problems because it does not enter into the curse of the branching factor of the CPF tree. MCFS does not think in-width on which child node to conduct the search as MCTS does. MCFS thinks in-depth along the best sequence found so far, and finds the best node of this sequence on which to fork a new sequence. MCFS is one of the first approaches that deals with CPF problems by optimizing time. NMCFS near-optimally solves the 16-puzzle and the 25-puzzle - puzzles without hole - but it is still surpassed by TOMPP. For congestion problems with four holes or two holes, NMCFS outperforms TASS and P&S. For large problems with many agents, large grids, and obstacles, our approach gives results with up to 400 agents and 200×200 gridsize. The cost of obtaining such results is computation time. MCFS is anytime and provides approximate solutions in limited time. Conversely to MCTS and A*, MCFS is not constrained by the huge branching factor of CPF problems. With sufficient time and memory, MCFS is complete. In finite time and with a finite memory, MCFS is not complete, and near-optimal only.

The current work can be investigated further in several directions. First, we aim at investigating the appropriate allocation of iterations in each nesting level. Secondly, studying the speed of convergence to optimality is an important perspective. Thirdly, we want to handle benchmarks [18]. Fourthly, assessing MCFS on other very high branching factor planning problems would be informative.

References

1. Auer, P., Cesa-Bianchi, N., Fischer, P.: Finite-time analysis of the multi-armed bandit problem. Mach. Learn. **47**(2–3), 235–256 (2002)

2. Browne, C., Powley, E., Whitehouse, D., Lucas, S., Cowling, P., Rohlfshagen, P., Tavener, S., Perez, D., Samothrakis, S., Colton, S.: A survey of Monte- Carlo tree search methods. IEEE TCIAIG **4**(1), 1–43 (2012)
3. Cazenave, T.: Nested Monte-Carlo Search. In: IJCAI (2011)
4. Coulom, R.: Efficient selectivity and backup operators in Monte-Carlo tree search. In: van den Herik, H.J., Ciancarini, P., Donkers, H.H.L.M.J. (eds.) CG 2006. LNCS, vol. 4630, pp. 72–83. Springer, Heidelberg (2007)
5. Khorshid, M.M.: Solving multi-agent pathfinding problems in polynomial time using tree decomposition. Master's thesis, University of Alberta (2011)
6. Khorshid, M.M., Holte, R.C., Sturtevant, N.R.: A polynomial-time algorithm for non-optimal multi-agent pathfinding. In: SoCS, pp. 76–83 (2011)
7. Kocsis, L., Szepesvári, C.: Bandit based Monte-Carlo planning. In: Fürnkranz, J., Scheffer, T., Spiliopoulou, M. (eds.) ECML 2006. LNCS (LNAI), vol. 4212, pp. 282–293. Springer, Heidelberg (2006)
8. Luna, R., Bekris, K.E.: Efficient and complete centralized multi-robot path planning. In: IROS (2011)
9. Luna, R., Bekris, K.E.: Push and swap: fast cooperative path-finding with completeness guarantees. In: IJCAI, pp. 294–300 (2011)
10. Pohl, I.: Bi-directional search. Mach. Intell. **6**, 127–140 (1971)
11. Ratner, D., Warmuth, M.: Finding a shortest solution for the Nx N-extension of the 15-puzzle is intractable. J. Symbolic Comput. **10**, 111–137 (1990)
12. Rosin, C.: Nested rollout policy adaptation for Monte Carlo- tree search. In: IJCAI, pp. 649–654 (2011)
13. Gelly, S., Silver, D.: Achieving master level play in 9x9 computer go. In: AAAI, pp. 1537–1540 (2008)
14. Sharon, G., Stern, R., Goldenberg, M., Felner, A.: The increasing cost tree search for optimal multi-agent pathfinding. In: IJCAI, pp. 662–667 (2011)
15. Silver, D.: Cooperative Pathfinding. AI Programming Wisdom (2006)
16. Standley, T.S.: Finding optimal solutions to cooperative pathfinding problems. In: AAAI (2010)
17. Standley, T.S., Korf, R.: Complete algorithms for cooperative pathfinding problems. In: IJCAI, pp. 668–673 (2011)
18. Sturtevant, N.: Benchmarks for grid-based pathfinding. IEEE TCIAIG **4**(2), 144–148 (2012)
19. Wang, K.-H.C., Botea, A.: MAPP: a scalable multi-agent path planning algorithm with tractability and completeness guarantees. JAIR **42**, 55–90 (2011)
20. Yu, J., LaValle, S.: Planning optimal paths for multiple agents on graphs. arXiv:1204.3830 (2012)
21. Yu, J., LaValle, S.: Time optimal multi-agent path planning on graphs. In: WoMP (2012)

Building Large Compressed PDBs
for the Sliding Tile Puzzle

Robert Döbbelin, Thorsten Schütt[(⊠)], and Alexander Reinefeld

Zuse Institute Berlin, Berlin, Germany
schuett@zib.de
http://www.zib.de

Abstract. The performance of heuristic search algorithms depends crucially on the effectiveness of the heuristic. A pattern database (PDB) is a powerful heuristic in the form of a pre-computed lookup table. Larger PDBs provide better bounds and thus allow more cut-offs in the search process. We computed 9-9-6, 9-8-7, and 8-8-8 PDBs for the 24-puzzle that are three orders of magnitude larger (up to 1.4 TB) than the 6-6-6-6 PDB. This was possible by performing a parallel breadth-first search in the compressed pattern space. Our experiments indicate an average 8-fold improvement of the 9-9-6 PDB over the 6-6-6-6 PDB on the 24-puzzle. Combining several large PDBs yields a 13-fold improvement.

1 Introduction

Heuristic search algorithms are widely used to solve combinatorial optimization problems. While traversing the problem space, the search process is guided by a heuristic function that provides a lower bound on the cost to a goal state. This allows to prune large parts of the search space and thus reduces the overall search effort. The more accurate the heuristic is, the more states can be pruned in the search. *Pattern Databases (PDBs)* are powerful heuristic functions in form of a lookup table. They store the exact solution of a relaxed version of the problem. The less the original problem is relaxed the larger is the size of the PDB and thereby the tighter are its bounds.

In this paper we present for the first time very large complete PDBs for the 24-puzzle: a 8-8-8 PDB with 122 GB, a 9-8-7 PDB with 733 GB, and a 9-9-6 PDB with 1381 GB. The largest one gave node savings by up to a factor of 37 compared to the 6-6-6-6 PDB [11].

We present a parallel algorithm that performs a breadth-first search in the compressed pattern space and thereby allows to compute very large PDBs on compute clusters with a modest amount of memory. The application of such large PDBs in heuristic search, however, requires a computer that allows to load the whole PDB into main memory. This can be as much as 1.4 TB for the 9-9-6 PDB, for example. While systems with more than 1 TB of main memory are not yet common, we believe that our work will help in studying the pruning-power of large PDBs.

T. Cazenave et al. (Eds.): CGW 2013, CCIS 408, pp. 16–27, 2014.
DOI: 10.1007/978-3-319-05428-5_2, © Springer International Publishing Switzerland 2014

The remainder of this paper is structured as follows. Section 2 sets the context of our work by reviewing relevant literature. Thereafter, PDBs are introduced in Sect. 3 and the algorithms and compressed data structures for generating large PDBs are presented in Sect. 4. In Sect. 5 we provide a statistical and empirical analysis and we summarize our work in Sect. 6.

2   Background

PDBs were first mentioned by Culberson and Schaeffer [3] and have been improved by several researchers. For instance, Felner *et al.* [8] presented additive PDBs in which the heuristic estimate is computed as the sum of the values of several smaller PDBs. The same authors also proposed a method for compressing a PDB for sliding tile puzzles by disregarding the blank tile and by computing the minimum distance over all possible blank positions. PDBs can be built with a backward breadth-first search over the complete state space. Large breadth-first searches have been used by Korf and Schultze [12] to expand the complete graph of the 15-puzzle for the first time. This was achieved by keeping the search front on disks and hiding the disk latency with multiple threads.

Orthogonal to additive PDBs is the idea of Holte *et al.* [9] to take the maximum h-value from several smaller PDBs instead of a single large one. They show that the accuracy of small h-values is especially important for reducing the number of expanded nodes.

Felner and Adler [6] use instance dependent PDBs to utilize large PDBs without completely creating them. They build on the observation of Zhou and Hansen [13] that only the nodes generated by the best-first search algorithm A* are needed in the pattern space to solve an individual instance. For each pattern of the given instance, Felner and Adler perform an A* search from the goal pattern towards the start pattern until the available memory is exhausted. This database is then used for the forward search. When h-values are missing, several smaller PDBs are used instead.

Breyer and Korf [1] apply a dense representation for problem spaces [2] to pattern databases. They store the heuristic estimates modulo three and restore the actual h-value during search. This results is a new compression technique using 1.6 bits per entry in the PDB.

Edelkamp *et al.* [4] created large symbolic pattern databases using an external breadth-first search with Binary Decision Diagrams (BDDs). They built a set of 7-tile PDBs for the 35-puzzle with a total size of 195 GB.

3   Pattern Databases

In this paper we are concerned with sliding tile puzzles. An instance of the $(n-1)$-puzzle can be described by n state variables, one for each tile. Each *state variable* describes the position of one specific tile in the tray. A *pattern* considers only a subset of the state variables; the remaining state variables are ignored. Hence, patterns abstract from the original problem by mapping several states to the same point in the pattern space. The number of ignored state variables can be used to control the information loss.

In the $(n-1)$-puzzle, a pattern is defined by a subset of the tiles. The position of the pattern tiles, the *pattern tile configuration*, and the blank defines a node in the pattern space. Move operations in the original problem can be analogously applied to nodes in the pattern space by moving either a pattern tile or a non-pattern tile, i.e. a *don't care tile*. Although we count the moves of don't cares, they are indistinguishable from each other. The size of the pattern space for a pattern with k tiles for the $(N-1)$-puzzle is $\frac{N!}{(N-k-1)!}$.

The number of moves needed to reach the goal in the pattern space can be used as an admissible heuristic for the move number in the original space. Because of the don't care tiles, a path in the original search space can only be longer than the corresponding path in the pattern space and hence the heuristic is admissible, i.e. non-overestimating.

To compute a PDB, we perform a backward breadth-first search from the goal to the start node and record for each visited node the distance from the goal.

3.1 Additive Pattern Databases

Because of space limitations, only small PDBs can be built. To get better heuristic estimates, several PDBs must be combined. However, with the above method, which also counts the movements of don't care tiles, we cannot simply add the h values of PDBs, even when the patterns are disjoint, because the same move would be counted several times. For additive PDBs [7] we only count the moves of pattern tiles.

The search space is mapped to the pattern space in the following way. Two states of the original space map to the same state in the pattern space, if the pattern tiles are in the same position and the two blank positions can be reached from each other by moving only don't care tiles. There is an edge between two nodes a and b in the pattern space if and only if there are two nodes c and d in the puzzle space where c maps to a and d maps to b and there is an edge between c and d.

Figure 1 shows an example for the 8-puzzle. Positions (a) and (b) map to the same state in the pattern space, because the blank positions are reachable from each other without moving pattern tiles. Positions (a) and (c), in contrast, do not map to the same state in the pattern space, because at least one pattern tile must be moved to shift the blank to the same position.

To further reduce the memory consumption, we compress the databases by the blank position as described in [7]. This is done by storing for any pattern-tile configuration, independent of the different blank positions, only the minimal distance from the goal node. For the three examples shown in Fig. 1 we only store one (the smallest) distance g in the PDB.

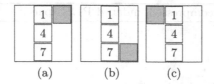

Fig. 1. Patterns with different blank positions (8-puzzle).

4   Building Compressed PDBs

When building large PDBs we ran into two limits: space and time. Not only do we need to keep the PDB itself in main memory, but also the Open and Closed lists must be stored. In Sect. 4.1 we describe a sequential algorithm and a compressed data structure for computing large PDBs. In Sect. 4.2 we describe a parallel implementation that uses the combined memory and compute capacity of a cluster as a single resource.

4.1   Sequential Algorithm

Our algorithm for building PDBs builds on ideas of [2]. To store the k-tile PDB, we use an array of $\frac{N!}{(N-k)!}$ elements, one entry for each state of the compressed pattern space. For our 9-tile PDB this results in $\frac{25!}{16!} = 741 \cdot 10^9$ entries. We use a perfect hash function to map a configuration of the pattern to this array. The hash function is reversible so that we can map an array index back to its pattern tile configuration. Each entry in the array is made up of three values: g, open_list and closed_list.

```
struct {
    byte g;
    byte open_list;
    byte closed_list;
} array_entry;
```

The variable g in Algorithm 1 stores for each entry the minimum g in which we found that state. Additionally, we need to store for each tuple of a pattern tile configuration and blank position whether it is in the Open or in the Closed list. This could be done by simply storing two bit strings of length $N - k$ in each PDB entry and setting the responsible bit whenever a new blank position is visited.

However, this simple approach can be improved to achieve a further data compression. A *blank partition* is a set of blank positions with a common pattern tile configuration where all blank positions are reachable from each other by only moving don't care tiles [5]. This is shown in Fig. 1: (a) and (b) belong to the same blank partition, while (a) and (c) do not. For patterns with 9 tiles, the pattern tile configurations have no more than 8 blank partitions. We can simply enumerate the blank partitions and only store one bit for each partition

---

Algorithm 1 BFS in compressed, indexed PDB space.

1: PDBArray A
2: initialize array
3: $expandedNodes = -1$;
4: $g = 1$;
5: **while** $expandedNodes \neq 0$ **do**
6:     $expandedNodes = 0$;
7:     **for** $i = 0 \rightarrow A.size - 1$ **do**
8:         **if** $A[i].open\_list = \emptyset$ **then**
9:             $continue$;
10:        **end if**
11:        $expandedNodes++$;
12:        $pattern = unindex(i)$;
13:        $blanks = unpackBlanks(A[i].open\_list)$;
14:        $succs = genSuccs(pattern, blanks)$;
15:        **for** $j = 0 \rightarrow succs.size - 1$ **do**
16:            $sIndex = index(succs[j])$;
17:            $rBlanks = reachableBlanks(succs[j])$;
18:            $pBlanks = packBlanks(rBlanks)$;
19:            $pBlanks \; -= A[sIndex].closed\_list$;
20:            $A[sIndex].open\_list \; += pBlanks$;
21:            $A[sIndex].g = min(A[sIndex].g, g)$;
22:        **end for**
23:        $A[i].closed\_list \; += A[i].open\_list$;
24:        $A[i].open\_list = \emptyset$;
25:    **end for**
26:    $g++$;
27: **end while**

---

in the `open_list` or `closed_list`. In the backward breadth-first search we used pre-computed lookup tables to map the blank positions to blank partitions. To build a PDB with up to 9 tiles, this scheme requires 3 bytes per state, one for g, `open_list`, and `closed_list`, respectively.

The breadth-first search over the pattern space is performed as follows (Algorithm 1): All `open_lists` and `closed_lists` are initialized with zeroes. The g for each state is set to the maximum value. For the initial state, the blank partition of the initial position is set in the `open_list`.

Then the array is scanned repeatedly (line 4). For each entry, we check if the Open list is empty (line 7). If not, we create the pattern tile configuration (line 11), extract all blank positions from the Open list (line 12) and finally generate the successors (line 13). For each successor, we calculate the index in the PDB (line 15), compress the blank positions (line 16-17) and update the successor's entry in the PDB (line 18–20). Note that backward steps are eliminated with the update. Finally, we update the `open_list` and `closed_list` of the current position. This is repeated until the complete pattern space has been visited. Note that the final PDB is stored using one byte per entry. The two bytes used for `open_list` and `closed_list` can be discarded.

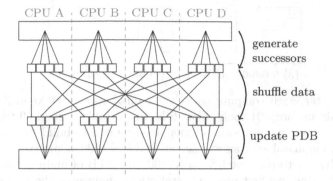

Fig. 2. Workflow of the parallel implementation.

4.2 Parallel Algorithm

For the parallel algorithm, we distribute the array (in disjoint partitions) over all compute nodes. To avoid imbalances in the work load, we do not assign contiguous parts to the nodes but use a hash function for assigning partitions of the array to the compute nodes. The parallel algorithm has the same structure as the sequential algorithm (see Fig. 2) but it needs additional communication to move the results to remote compute nodes.

For each g, first each node scans its part of the array and generates the successors as described in Algorithm 1. But instead of directly updating the PDB, each node collects the successors locally. In the shuffle phase (Fig. 2), these successors are sent to the nodes storing the corresponding partitions in the PDB. Finally, the PDB is updated locally.

Dealing with Memory Limitations. The parallel implementation requires more memory than the sequential algorithm, because successors are cached locally before they are stored in the array. The generated successors in a large search front could exceed the available memory of a compute node. Thus, we implemented the following scheme to bound the overall memory consumption. If a processor is about to run out of memory, it stops scanning the array and raises a flag. In this case all processor mark updates to the Open lists in the BFS array as new, g is not incremented and the array is scanned again. Then only those Open lists are considered, which are not marked as new. Once all processors succeeded scanning the array, the flag is removed from all Open lists and the algorithm proceeds with the next g.

5 Evaluation

We used the presented parallel algorithm to build three large PDBs, 8-8-8, 9-8-7, and 9-9-6, with sizes of 122 GB, 733 GB and 1381 GB, respectively. For comparison, the 6-6-6-6 PDB has a size of only 488 MB.

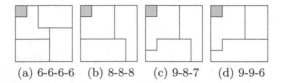

(a) 6-6-6-6   (b) 8-8-8   (c) 9-8-7   (d) 9-9-6

In our cluster, each compute node has 2 quad-core Intel Xeon X5570 with 48 GB of main memory. It took about 6 hours to build a single 9-tile PDB on 255 nodes. The maximum amount of memory required to build such a PDB was 3 TB. For the empirical analysis we used an SGI UV 1000, a large shared-memory machine with 64 octo-core Intel Xeon X7560 and 2 TB of main memory.

In the following, we first present a statistical analysis of the performance of our PDBs on a large number of randomly generated positions. Thereafter we show the performance on Korf's set of random 24-puzzle instances [12]. In both cases, we used mirroring [3] to improve the accuracy of the heuristics.

5.1   Statistical Evaluation

We created 100,000,000 random instances of the 24-puzzle and recorded the h-values obtained with the 6-6-6-6, 8-8-8, 9-8-7, and 9-9-6 PDB. Figure 3 shows the cumulative distribution, i.e. the probability $P(X \leq h)$, that the heuristic value for a random state is less or equal to h. The higher the h-value, the better the pruning power of the heuristic. This is because all heuristics are admissible, i.e. they never overestimate the goal distance. Higher h-values represent therefore tighter bounds on the true value. As can be seen in Fig. 3, all graphs lie close together and their order corresponds to the size and pruning power of the PDBs. Interestingly, the new PDBs are distinctively better than the 6-6-6-6 PDB (see the dashed line).

Note that the increased number of small h-values is especially important for the performance of the heuristic [9]. Figure 4 shows a magnification of the lower left corner of the data in Fig. 3. It can be seen that all curves are clearly distinct and that the large PDBs provide a considerable improvement over the 6-6-6-6 PDB.

Table 1 lists the average, minimum, and maximum values. In accordance with Fig. 3, larger PDBs return on average a higher h-value. Checking the extreme values reveals an interesting fact: While the minimum value of the 9-9-6 PDB is 4 moves higher than the lowest value of the 6-6-6-6, its maximum value is only

Table 1. Average, minimum and maximum h-values of 100,000,000 random instances.

PDB	Size [GB]	Avg. h	Min. h	Max. h
6-6-6-6	0.488	81.85	40	115
8-8-8	122	82.84	40	116
9-8-7	733	83.10	43	116
9-9-6	1381	83.56	44	116

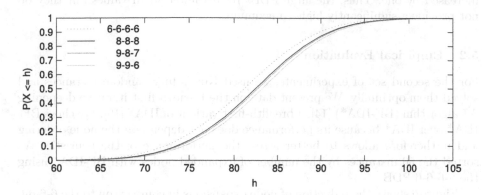

Fig. 3. Cumulative distribution of h-values of 100,000,000 random samples.

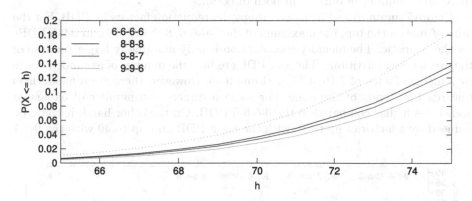

Fig. 4. Magnification of the lower left corner of Fig. 3.

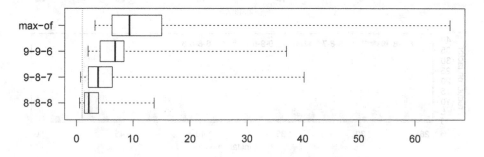

Fig. 5. Reduction factors compared to 6-6-6-6 PDB.

increased by one. Thus, the large PDBs return fewer small values but they do not provide a significantly higher maximum.

5.2 Empirical Evaluation

For the second set of experiments, we used Korf's fifty random instances and solved them optimally. We present data on the breadth-first iterative deepening A* algorithm (BF-IDA*) [14], a breadth-first variant of IDA* [10]. We chose BF-IDA* over IDA* because its performance does not depend on the node ordering and it therefore allows to better assess the performance of the heuristic. We sorted the 50 instances by the number of expanded nodes with BF-IDA* using the 6-6-6-6 PDB.

Figure 6 shows the reduction of node expansions in comparison to the 6-6-6-6 PDB. For each bar we divided the nodes expanded by the 6-6-6-6 PDB by that of the other PDBs. In general, larger PDBs tend to perform better than smaller ones and the gain seems to be independent from the problem difficulty. However, there are a number of outliers in both directions.

Figure 5 summarizes Fig. 6 and groups the reduction factors by PDB. For the *max-of* line on the top, the maximum of the 6-6-6-6, 8-8-8, 9-8-7 and 9-9-6 PDBs for the heuristic. The memory consumption is only marginally larger because of the overlapping partitions. The four PDBs reduce the number of expanded nodes by a median factor of 2.16, 3.86, 6.81 and 9.36. However, there are some outliers towards both ends of the scale. For some instances the number of expanded nodes was higher compared to the 6-6-6-6 PDB. On the other hand, it could be reduced by a factor of up to 10 with the 8-8-8 PDB and up to 40 with the 9-8-7

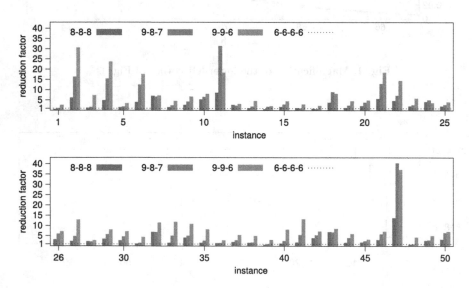

Fig. 6. Reduction factor to 6-6-6-6 PDB on Korf's random set (ordered by IDA* nodes) using BF-IDA*.

and 9-9-6 PDBs. The standard deviation seems to slightly increase with the size of the heuristic.

Table 2 in the Appendix shows the detailed results for each problem instance. The first column gives the Id used in [12] and the second column states the length d of the shortest path. The number of expanded nodes with the individual PDBs are listed in columns three to seven. Columns eight to eleven give the reduction factor of the 8-8-8, 9-8-7, 9-9-6, and max-of PDBs relative to the 6-6-6-6 PDB.

6 Conclusion

We presented an efficient parallel algorithm and a compact data structure that allowed us to compute for the first time very large compressed PDBs. The parallel algorithm utilizes the aggregated memory of multiple parallel computers to compute and store the PDB in the main memory.

We computed three additive PDBs for the 24-puzzle, an 8-8-8, 9-8-7 and 9-9-6 PDB. To the best of our knowledge, these are the largest PDBs reported for this domain.

The 9-9-6 PDB gives on average an 8-fold node reduction compared to a 6-6-6-6 PDB on Korf's random instances of the 24-puzzle. We observed a high variance on the reduction rate, which ranges from 2x to 37x savings (Table 2). Hence, we suggest to use the maximum over several additive PDBs in practice. This is feasible, because multiple additive PDBs do not proportionally increase the memory consumption. This is because the same PDB can be utilized by multiple additive PDBs. As an example, the same 9 PDB can be used in both of our 9-9-6 PDB and the 9-8-7 PDB.

Acknowledgments. This work was partly supported by the EU project CONTRAIL, the DFG project FFMK and the North German Supercomputer Alliance HLRN.

Appendix

Table 2. Expanded nodes of all 50 random instances (r_1: 6-6-6-6 / 8-8-8, r_2: 6-6-6-6 / 9-8-7 , r_3: 6-6-6-6 / 9-9-6, r_4: 6-6-6-6 / max-of).

Id d	6-6-6-6	8-8-8	9-8-7	9-9-6	max-of	r_1	r_2	r_3	r_4
40 82	26,320,497	49,291,000	26,655,910	10,486,000	7,166,383	0.53	0.99	2.51	3.67
38 96	58,097,633	9,577,883	3,573,949	1,906,127	1,638,334	6.07	16.26	30.48	35.46
25 81	127,949,696	118,780,897	85,141,009	17,658,986	15,217,162	1.08	1.50	7.25	8.41
44 93	181,555,996	37,853,812	11,869,090	7,686,937	5,547,600	4.80	15.30	23.62	32.73
32 97	399,045,498	281,515,091	232,222,028	117,317,314	67,570,393	1.42	1.72	3.40	5.91
28 98	450,493,295	114,571,662	36,263,727	25,552,985	19,743,793	3.93	12.42	17.63	22.82
22 95	581,539,254	82,503,279	88,652,504	81,038,427	37,858,513	7.05	6.56	7.18	15.36

(continued)

Table 2. (continued)

Id d	6-6-6-6	8-8-8	9-8-7	9-9-6	max-of	r_1	r_2	r_3	r_4
36 90	603,580,192	408,261,989	252,309,866	133,482,919	95,563,302	1.48	2.39	4.52	6.32
30 92	661,835,606	256,431,250	158,409,200	99,557,684	52,338,447	2.58	4.18	6.65	12.65
1 95	1,059,622,872	199,198,406	163,950,295	133,060,463	63,948,759	5.32	6.46	7.96	16.57
29 88	1,090,385,785	128,886,129	34,814,333	59,609,938	21,223,415	8.46	31.32	18.29	51.38
37 100	1,646,715,005	628,890,120	725,323,664	542,573,720	331,223,844	2.62	2.27	3.04	4.97
16 96	1,783,144,872	1,729,554,795	966,783,772	387,360,939	296,519,726	1.03	1.84	4.60	6.01
5 100	1,859,102,197	3,125,977,623	1,078,990,063	905,861,248	565,263,022	0.59	1.72	2.05	3.27
13 101	1,979,587,555	1,181,771,575	690,327,991	444,476,728	268,475,464	1.68	2.87	4.45	7.37
47 92	4,385,270,986	3,825,636,827	4,520,442,316	1,479,759,728	960,463,883	1.15	0.97	2.96	4.57
3 97	4,805,007,493	5,699,072,723	6,731,407,433	2,146,564,697	1,113,194,453	0.84	0.71	2.24	4.32
4 98	5,154,861,019	1,361,290,863	581,368,420	632,299,449	370,467,747	3.79	8.87	8.15	13.91
26 105	6,039,700,647	4,993,857,550	2,525,926,189	1,337,993,889	955,364,988	1.21	2.39	4.51	6.32
31 99	7,785,405,374	3,653,831,114	2,058,364,161	1,622,465,469	992,726,542	2.13	3.78	4.80	7.84
27 99	7,884,559,441	1,415,859,414	611,960,188	432,345,846	337,466,232	5.57	12.88	18.24	23.23
41 106	8,064,453,928	1,737,010,534	1,123,917,776	561,944,277	455,028,148	4.64	7.18	14.35	17.72
43 104	8,816,151,498	4,378,714,353	3,498,876,258	1,532,474,999	1,090,696,435	2.01	2.52	5.75	8.08
6 101	9,810,208,759	2,397,434,227	1,982,606,973	2,739,184,006	1,053,141,115	4.09	4.95	3.58	9.32
49 100	11,220,738,849	5,526,627,744	4,160,235,910	2,792,736,271	1,587,674,537	2.03	2.70	4.02	7.07
45 101	17,068,061,084	5,614,562,048	2,909,124,921	2,408,543,192	1,339,279,458	3.04	5.87	7.09	12.74
20 92	20,689,215,063	9,014,702,404	4,354,383,611	1,615,310,063	1,378,812,797	2.30	4.75	12.81	15.01
46 100	21,674,806,323	9,872,851,915	10,304,210,129	8,017,940,089	3,402,288,275	2.20	2.10	2.70	6.37
19 106	22,761,173,348	6,759,987,121	4,019,764,127	2,836,304,399	2,125,081,076	3.37	5.66	8.02	10.71
35 98	23,049,423,391	8,584,994,059	4,998,934,055	3,208,321,325	2,369,834,229	2.68	4.61	7.18	9.73
7 104	27,686,193,468	26,781,188,637	19,232,502,973	6,429,879,587	4,395,653,789	1.03	1.44	4.31	6.30
8 108	29,575,219,906	4,318,849,565	4,366,429,730	2,609,051,057	1,727,994,805	6.85	6.77	11.34	17.12
39 104	34,198,605,172	22,810,919,845	6,881,101,921	2,912,577,301	2,428,595,642	1.50	4.97	11.74	14.08
42 108	37,492,323,962	9,339,335,844	7,508,532,598	3,490,897,448	2,697,310,294	4.01	4.99	10.74	13.09
24 107	38,272,741,957	25,802,863,114	15,170,752,402	4,724,091,699	3,837,236,834	1.48	2.52	8.10	9.97
2 96	40,161,477,151	29,318,072,174	28,011,360,591	14,446,211,551	8,963,348,921	1.37	1.43	2.78	4.48
15 103	52,178,879,610	26,951,022,561	18,771,225,751	9,741,418,794	8,075,823,446	1.94	2.78	5.36	6.46
23 104	54,281,904,788	36,611,741,317	32,729,241,923	11,103,574,065	8,930,804,356	1.48	1.66	4.89	6.08
48 107	58,365,224,981	99,614,525,233	68,013,167,519	19,890,964,633	12,563,246,704	0.59	0.86	2.93	4.65
34 102	59,225,710,222	49,923,377,951	24,336,781,035	7,384,409,074	5,346,161,078	1.19	2.43	8.02	11.08
12 109	76,476,143,041	43,132,155,298	14,260,876,794	5,820,163,959	4,265,458,902	1.77	5.36	13.14	17.93
21 103	98,083,647,769	25,411,173,479	18,746,227,139	13,731,206,789	8,402,416,300	3.86	5.23	7.14	11.67
18 110	126,470,260,027	18,375,847,744	18,999,810,842	15,070,620,942	7,809,249,544	6.88	6.66	8.39	16,19
9 113	132,599,245,368	82,839,919,151	33,749,539,711	22,489,080,304	16,927,179,096	1.60	3.93	5.90	7.83
33 106	134,103,676,989	77,163,409,262	57,402,766,270	42,219,474,099	25,271,466,707	1.74	2.34	3.18	5.31
17 109	143,972,316,747	49,516,974,145	25,000,824,805	20,405,484,237	15,304,298,302	2.91	5.76	7.06	9.41
11 106	309,253,017,124	22,602,670,676	7,683,989,291	8,343,197,181	4,678,739,173	13.68	40.25	37.07	66.10
14 111	312,885,453,572	419,699,251,120	360,169,788,945	74,779,904,961	63,056,188,490	0.75	0.87	4.18	4.96
10 114	525,907,193,133	207,752,246,775	192,243,603,386	105,311,763,457	63,629,118,230	2.53	2.74	4.99	8.27
50 113	1,067,321,687,213	334,283,260,227	168,384,195,109	152,720,707,871	100,026,128,248	3.19	6.34	6.99	10.67
Average	71,004,578,707.12	33,908,766,050.50	23,611,990,572.06	11,599,129,942.46	7,794,424,738.66	3.00	5.74	8.37	12.85
Median	14,144,399,966.50	5,570,594,896.00	4,257,309,760.50	2,508,797,124.50	1,359,046,127.50	2.16	3.86	6.81	9.36

References

1. Breyer, T.M., Korf, R.E.: 1.6-bit pattern databases. In: AAAI (2010)
2. Cooperman, G., Finkelstein, L.: New methods for using Cayley graphs in interconnection networks. Discrete Appl. Math. **37**, 95–118 (1992)
3. Culberson, J.C., Schaeffer, J.: Pattern databases. Comput. Intell. **14**(3), 318–334 (1998)
4. Edelkamp, S., Jabbar, S., Kissmann, P.: Scaling search with pattern databases. In: Peled, D.A., Wooldridge, M.J. (eds.) MoChArt 2008. LNCS, vol. 5348, pp. 49–64. Springer, Heidelberg (2009)

5. Felner, A.: Improving search techniques and using them on different environments. Ph.D. thesis (2001)
6. Felner, A., Adler, A.: Solving the 24 Puzzle with instance dependent pattern databases. In: Zucker, J.-D., Saitta, L. (eds.) SARA 2005. LNCS (LNAI), vol. 3607, pp. 248–260. Springer, Heidelberg (2005)
7. Felner, A., Korf, R.E., Hanan, S.: Additive pattern database heuristics. J. Artif. Intell. Res. **22**, 279–318 (2004)
8. Felner, A., Meshulam, R., Holte, R.C., Korf, R.E.: Compressing pattern databases. In: AAAI, pp. 638–643 (2004)
9. Holte, R.C., Newton, J., Felner, A., Meshulam, R., Furcy, D.: Multiple pattern databases. In: Proceedings of the Fourteenth International Conference on Automated Planning and Scheduling (ICAPS-04), pp. 122–131 (2004)
10. Korf, R.E.: Depth-first iterative-deepening an optimal admissible tree search. Artif. Intell. **27**(1), 97–109 (1985)
11. Korf, R.E., Felner, A.: Disjoint pattern database heuristics. Artif. Intell. **134**(1–2), 9–22 (2002)
12. Korf, R.E., Schultze, P.: Large-scale parallel breadth-first search. In: Proceedings of the National Conference on Artificial Intelligence, vol. 20, pp. 1380–1385. AAAI Press/MIT Press (2005)
13. Zhou, R., Hansen, E.A.: Space-efficient memory-based heuristics. In: Proceedings of the National Conference on Artificial Intelligence, pp. 677–682. AAAI Press/MIT Press (2004)
14. Zhou, R., Hansen, E.A.: Breadth-first heuristic search. Artif. Intell. **170**(4–5), 385–408 (2006)

Monte Carlo Tree Search in Simultaneous Move Games with Applications to Goofspiel

Marc Lanctot[1](✉), Viliam Lisý[2], and Mark H.M. Winands[1]

[1] Department of Knowledge Engineering, Maastricht University,
Maastricht, The Netherlands
[2] Department of Computer Science, Czech Technical University in Prague,
Praha, Czech Republic
{marc.lanctot,m.winands}@maastrichtuniversity.nl, lisy@agents.fel.cvut.cz

Abstract. Monte Carlo Tree Search (MCTS) has become a widely popular sampled-based search algorithm for two-player games with perfect information. When actions are chosen simultaneously, players may need to mix between their strategies. In this paper, we discuss the adaptation of MCTS to simultaneous move games. We introduce a new algorithm, Online Outcome Sampling (OOS), that approaches a Nash equilibrium strategy over time. We compare both head-to-head performance and exploitability of several MCTS variants in Goofspiel. We show that regret matching and OOS perform best and that all variants produce less exploitable strategies than UCT.

1 Introduction

Monte Carlo Tree Search (MCTS) is a simulation-based search technique often used in extensive-form games [9,16]. Having first seen practical success in computer Go [13], MCTS has since been applied successfully to general game playing, real-time and continuous domains, multi-player games, single-player games, imperfect information games, computer games, and more [4].

Despite its empirical success, formal guarantees of convergence of a MCTS to the optimal action choice were analyzed only for a MCTS variant called UCT [16], in the case of two-player zero-sum perfect-information sequential (turn-taking) games. In this paper, we focus on MCTS in zero-sum games with perfect information and simultaneous moves. We argue that a good search algorithm for this class of games should converge to a Nash equilibrium (NE) of the game, which is not the case for a variant of UCT [25], commonly used in this setting. Other variants of MCTS, which may converge to NE were suggested [26], but this property was never proven or experimentally evaluated.

In this paper, we introduce Online Outcome Sampling (OOS), a MCTS algorithm derived from Monte Carlo counterfactual regret minimization [17], which provably converges to NE in this class of games. We provide experimental evidence that OOS and several other variants of MCTS, based on Exp3 and Regret matching, also converge to NE in a smaller version of the card game Goofspiel.

T. Cazenave et al. (Eds.): CGW 2013, CCIS 408, pp. 28–43, 2014.
DOI: 10.1007/978-3-319-05428-5_3, © Springer International Publishing Switzerland 2014

In addition, we compare the head-to-head performance of five different MCTS variants in full-size Goofspiel. Since Goofspiel has recently been solved [21], we use the optimal minimax values of every state to estimate the exploitability (i.e., worst-case regret) of the strategies used in the full game. The results show that regret matching and an optimized form of OOS (OOS$^+$), which have never been used in context of MCTS, produce the strongest Goofspiel players.

1.1 Related Work

The first application of MCTS to simultaneous move games was in general game playing (GGP) [11] programs. The Cadiaplayer [12] using a strategy we describe as DUCT in Subsect. 3.1 was the top performing player of the GGP competition between 2007 and 2009. Despite this success, Shafiei *et al.* [25] provide a counter-example showing that this straightforward application of UCT does not converge to NE even in the simplest simultaneous move games and that a player playing a NE can exploit this strategy. Another variant of UCT, which has been applied to the simultaneous move game Tron [24], builds the tree as if the players were moving sequentially giving one of the player unrealistic informational advantage. This approach also cannot converge to NE in general.

For this reason, other variants of MCTS were considered for simultaneous move games. Teytaud and Flory [26] describe a search algorithm for games with short-term imperfect information, which are a generalization of simultaneous move games. Their algorithm uses Exp3 (see Subsect. 3.2) for the simultaneous moves and was shown to work well in the Internet card game Urban Rivals. A more thorough investigation of different selection policies including UCB, UCB1-Tuned, ϵ-greedy, Exp3, and more is reported in the game of Tron [20]. We show a similar head-to-head performance comparison for Goofspiel in Sect. 4 and we add an analysis of convergence to NE.

Finnsson applied simultaneous move MCTS to several games, including small games of Goofspiel [12, Chapter 6]. This work focused mainly on pruning provably dominated moves. Their algorithm uses solutions to linear programs in the framework of Score-Bounded MCTS [6] to extend the ideas of MCTS-Solver [27] to simultaneous move games. Saffidine *et al.* [23] and Bosansky *et al.* [3] recently described methods for $\alpha\beta$ pruning in simultaneous move games, and also applied their algorithms to simplified Goofspiel. Our work differs in that our algorithm is built with the simulation-based search framework of Monte Carlo Tree Search (MCTS), which is more suitable for larger games with difficult evaluation of the quality of intermediate game states.

The ideas presented in this paper are different than MMCTS and IS-MCTS [2,10] in the sense that the imperfect information that arises in simultaneous move games is rather short term because it only occurs between state transitions. In our case game trees may include chance events, but the outcomes of the chance events are observable by each player. As a result, techniques such as backward induction [5,21,22] are applicable, and search algorithms can be seen as sample-based approximations of these solvers.

2 Simultaneous Move Games

A finite game with simultaneous moves and chance can be described by a tuple $(\mathcal{N}, \mathcal{S} = \mathcal{D} \cup \mathcal{C} \cup \mathcal{Z}, \mathcal{A}, \mathcal{T}, \Delta_c, u_i, s_0)$. The player set $\mathcal{N} = \{1, 2, c\}$ contains player labels, where c denotes the chance player and by convention a player is denoted $i \in \mathcal{N}$. $\mathcal{S}$ is a set of states, with $\mathcal{Z}$ denoting the terminal states, $\mathcal{D}$ the states where players make decisions, and $\mathcal{C}$ the possibly empty set of states where chance events occur. $\mathcal{A} = \mathcal{A}_1 \times \mathcal{A}_2$ is the set of joint actions of individual players. We denote $\mathcal{A}_i(s)$ the actions available to player i in state $s \in \mathcal{S}$. The transition function $\mathcal{T} : \mathcal{S} \times \mathcal{A}_1 \times \mathcal{A}_2 \mapsto \mathcal{S}$ defines the successor state given a current state and actions for both players. $\Delta_c : \mathcal{C} \mapsto \Delta(\mathcal{S})$ describes a probability distribution over possible successor states of the chance event. The utility functions $u_i : \mathcal{Z} \mapsto [v_{\min}, v_{\max}] \subseteq \mathbb{R}$ gives the utility of player i, with v_{min} and $v_{\max}$ denoting the minimum and maximum possible utility respectively. We assume constant-sum games: $\forall z \in \mathcal{Z}, u_1(z) = k - u_2(z)$. The game begins in an initial state s_0.

A *matrix game* is a single step simultaneous move game with action sets $\mathcal{A}_1$ and $\mathcal{A}_2$. Each entry in the matrix A_{rc} where $(r, c) \in A_1 \times A_2$ corresponds to a payoff (to player 1) if row r is chosen by player 1 and column c by player 2. For example, in Matching Pennies, each player has two actions (heads or tails). The row player receives a payoff of 1 if both players choose the same action and 0 if they do not match. Two-player simultaneous move games are sometimes called *stacked matrix games* because at every state s there is a joint action set $\mathcal{A}_1(s) \times \mathcal{A}_2(s)$ that either leads to a terminal state or (possibly after a chance transition) to a subgame which is itself another stacked matrix game.

A *behavioral strategy* for player i is a mapping from states $s \in \mathcal{S}$ to a probability distribution over the actions $\mathcal{A}_i(s)$, denoted $\sigma_i(s)$. Given a profile $\sigma = (\sigma_1, \sigma_2)$, define the probability of reaching a terminal state z under σ as $\pi^\sigma(z) = \pi_1(z)\pi_2(z)\pi_c(z)$, where each $\pi_i(z)$ is a product of probabilities of the actions taken by player i along the path to z (c being chance's probabilities). Define Σ_i to be the set of behavioral strategies for player i. A Nash equilibrium profile in this case is a pair of behavioral strategies optimizing

$$V^* = \max_{\sigma_1 \in \Sigma_1} \min_{\sigma_2 \in \Sigma_2} \mathbb{E}_{z \sim \sigma}[u_1(z)] = \max_{\sigma_1 \in \Sigma_1} \min_{\sigma_2 \in \Sigma_2} \sum_{z \in Z} \pi^\sigma(z) u_1(z). \qquad (1)$$

In other words, none of the players can improve their utility by deviating unilaterally. For example, the Matching Pennies matrix game has a single state and the only equilibrium strategy is to mix equally between both actions, i.e., play with a *mixed strategy* (distribution) of $(0.5, 0.5)$ giving an expected payoff of $V^* = 0.5$. If the strategies also optimize Eq. 1 in each subgame starting in an arbitrary state, the equilibrium strategy is termed subgame perfect.

In two-player constant sum games a (subgame perfect) Nash equilibrium strategy is often considered to be optimal. It guarantees the payoff of at least V^* against any opponent. Any non-equilibrium strategy has its nemesis, which will make it win less than V^* in expectation. Moreover, subgame perfect NE strategy can earn more than V^* against weak opponents. After the opponent

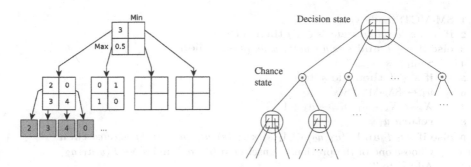

Fig. 1. Examples of a two-player simultaneous game without chance nodes (left) which has Matching Pennies as a subgame, and a portion of 3-card Goofspiel including chance nodes (right). The dark squares are terminal states. The values shown are optimal values that could be obtained by backward induction. Note: the left figure is taken from [3] and provided by Branislav Bosansky.

makes a sub-optimal move, the strategy will never allow it to gain the loss back. The value V^* is known as the minimax-optimal value of the game and is the same for every equilibrium profile by von Neumann's minimax theorem.

A two-player simultaneous move game is a specific type of two-player imperfect information extensive-form game. In imperfect information games, states are grouped into *information sets*: two states $s, s' \in I$ if the player to act at I cannot distinguish which of these states the game is currently in. Any simultaneous move game can be modeled using an information set to represent a half-completed transition, i.e., $\mathcal{T}(s, a_1, ?)$ or $\mathcal{T}(s, ?, a_2)$.

The model described above is similar to a two-player finite horizon Markov Game [19] with chance events. Examples of such games are depicted in Fig. 1.

3   Simultaneous Move Monte Carlo Tree Search

Monte Carlo Tree Search (MCTS) [9,16] is a simulation-based search algorithm often used in game trees. The main idea is to iteratively run simulations to a terminal state, incrementally growing a tree rooted at the current state. In its simplest form, the tree is initially empty and a single leaf is added each iteration. The nodes in the tree represent game states (decision nodes) or chance events (chance nodes). Each simulation starts by visiting nodes in the tree, selecting (or sampling) which actions to take based on information maintained in the node, and then consequently transitioning to the successor states. When a node is visited whose immediate children are not all in the tree, the node is expanded by adding a new leaf to the tree. Then, a rollout policy is applied from the new leaf to a terminal state. The outcome of the simulation is then back-propagated to all the nodes that were visited during the simulation.

In Simultaneous Move MCTS (SM-MCTS), the main difference is that a joint action is selected. The convergence to an optimal strategy depends critically on

1 SM-MCTS(node s)
2 **if** s *is a terminal state ($s \in \mathcal{Z}$)* **then return** $u_1(s)$
3 **else if** $s \in T$ **and** s *is a chance node ($s \in \mathcal{C}$)* **then**
4   Sample $s' \sim \Delta_c(s)$
5   **if** $s' \notin T$ **then** add s' to T
6      $u_1 \leftarrow$ SM-MCTS(s')
7      $X_s \leftarrow X_s + u_1; \; n_s \leftarrow n_s + 1$
8   **return** u_1
9 **else if** $s \in T$ **and** $\exists (a_1, a_2) \in \mathcal{A}_1(s) \times \mathcal{A}_2(s)$ *not previously selected* **then**
10   Choose one of the previously unselected (a_1, a_2) and $s' \leftarrow \mathcal{T}(s, a_1, a_2)$
11   Add s' to T
12     $u_1 \leftarrow$ Rollout(s')
13     $X_{s'} \leftarrow X_{s'} + u_1; \; n_{s'} \leftarrow n_{s'} + 1$
14     $\underline{\text{Update}}(s, a_1, a_2, u_1)$
15   **return** u_1
16 $(a_1, a_2) \leftarrow \underline{\text{Select}}(s)$
17 $s' \leftarrow \mathcal{T}(s, a_1, a_2)$
18 $u_1 \leftarrow$ SM-MCTS(s')
19 $\underline{\text{Update}}(s, a_1, a_2, u_1)$
20 **return** u_1

Algorithm 1: Simultaneous Move Monte Carlo Tree Search

the selection and update policies applied, which are not as straightforward as in purely sequential games. Algorithm 1 describes a single simulation of SM-MCTS. T represents the MCTS tree in which each state is represented by one node. Every node s maintains a cumulative reward sum over all simulations through it, X_s, and a visit count n_s, both initially set to 0. As with standard MCTS, when a state is visited these values are incremented, in the same way on lines 7 and 13, and in the node updates on lines 14 and 19. As seen in Fig. 1, a matrix of references to the children is maintained at each decision node.

Chance nodes are explicitly added to the tree and handled between lines 3 and 7, which is skipped in games without chance events since $|\mathcal{C}| = 0$. At a chance node s, $\bar{X}_s = X_s/n_s$ represents the mean value of the chance node and corresponding joint action at the parent of s. This mean value at chance nodes approximates the expected value (weighted sum) that would be computed by backward induction or a depth-limited search algorithm.

At a decision node s, the estimated values $\bar{X}_{s'}$ of the children nodes $s' = \mathcal{T}(s, a_1, a_2)$ over all joint actions form an estimated payoff matrix for node s. The critical parts of the algorithm are the updates on lines 14 and 19 and the selection on line 16. Each variant below will describe a different way to select a joint action and update a decision node.

In practice, there are several optimizations to the base algorithm that might be desirable. For example, if a game has a large branching factor, it may take many iterations for the expansion condition and consequence in lines 9 to 10 to fill up the matrix before switching to a selection policy. The matrix can instead be filled such that at least one action has been taken from each row and one from each column before switching to the selection policy. Since DUCT and Exp3 do not require values for each entry in the matrix, this could reduce the number of simulations before switching to $|\mathcal{A}_1(s)| + |\mathcal{A}_2(s)|$ from $|\mathcal{A}_1(s)||\mathcal{A}_2(s)|$. The use of progressive widening [7,8] may also lead to deeper searches. In this paper, the implementation for experiments is based on the pseudo-code presented in Algorithm 1.

3.1 Decoupled UCT

In Decoupled UCT (DUCT) [11], each player i maintains separate reward sums $X^i_{s,a}$ and visit counts $n^i_{s,a}$ for their own action set $a \in \mathcal{A}_i(s)$. When a joint action needs to be selected on line 16, each player selects an action that maximizes the UCB value over their reward estimates independently:

$$a_i = \operatorname*{argmax}_{a \in A_i(s)} \left\{ \bar{X}^i_{s,a} + C_i \sqrt{\frac{\ln n_s}{n_{s,a}}} \right\}, \text{ where } \bar{X}^i_{s,a} = \frac{X^i_{s,a}}{n_{s,a}} \tag{2}$$

The update policy increases the rewards and visit counts for each player i: $X^i_{s,a_i} \leftarrow X^i_{s,a_i} + u_i$, and $n_{s,a_i} \leftarrow n_{s,a_i} + 1$.

While references to children nodes in the MCTS tree are maintained in a matrix, each player *decouples* the values and estimates from the joint actions space. In other words, for some state s, each player maintains their own tables of values. For example, suppose the actions sets are $\mathcal{A}_1(s) = \{a, b, c\}$ and $\mathcal{A}_2(s) = \{A, B, C\}$, then the information maintained by at state s is depicted in Fig. 2. Many of the other selection policies also maintain values separately, and some use jointly maintained values.

After the simulations, a move is chosen that maximizes $\bar{X}^i_{s,a_i}$ for the searching player i. Alternatively, one can choose to play a mixed (i.e., randomized) strategy by normalizing the visit counts. We call the former DUCT(max) and the latter DUCT(mix).

3.2 Exp3

In Exp3 [1], each player maintains an estimate of the sum of rewards, denoted $\hat{x}^i_{s,a}$, and visit counts $n^i_{s,a}$ for each of their actions. The joint action selected on

Player 1			Player 2		
Action	Reward Sum	Visit Count	Action	Reward Sum	Visit Count
a	$X^1_{s,a}$	$n_{s,a}$	A	$X^2_{s,A}$	$n_{s,A}$
b	$X^1_{s,b}$	$n_{s,b}$	B	$X^2_{s,B}$	$n_{s,B}$
c	$X^1_{s,c}$	$n_{s,c}$	C	$X^2_{s,C}$	$n_{s,C}$

Fig. 2. Decoupled values maintained in the tree at a node representing state s.

line 16 is composed of an action independently selected for each player based on the probability distribution. This probability of sampling action a_i is

$$\sigma_i^t(s, a_i) = \frac{(1 - \gamma) \exp(\eta w_{s,a_i}^i)}{\sum_{a_j \in \mathcal{A}_i(s)} \exp(\eta w_{s,a_j}^i)} + \frac{\gamma}{|\mathcal{A}_i(s)|}, \text{ where} \tag{3}$$

$$\eta = \frac{\gamma}{|\mathcal{A}_i(s)|}, \text{ and } w_{s,a}^i = \hat{x}_{s,a}^i - \max_{a' \in \mathcal{A}_i(s)} \hat{x}_{s,a'}^i.$$

Here, the reason to use $w_{s,a}^i$ is for numerical stability in the implementation. The action selected by normalizing over the maximum value will be identical to the action chosen without normalizing.

The update after selecting actions (a_1, a_2) and obtaining a simulation result (u_1, u_2) updates the visits count and adds to the corresponding reward sum estimates the reward divided by the probability that the action was played by the player using

$$n_{s,a_i} \leftarrow n_{s,a_i} + 1, \quad \hat{x}_{s,a_i}^i \leftarrow \hat{x}_{s,a_i}^i + \frac{u_i}{\sigma_i^t(s, a_i)}.$$

Dividing the value by the probability of selecting the corresponding action makes $\hat{x}_{s,a}^i$ estimate the sum of rewards over all iterations, not only the once where a_i was selected.

Since these values and strategies are maintained separately for each player, Exp3 is decoupled in the same sense as DUCT, storing values separately as depicted by Fig. 2.

The mixed strategy used by player i after the simulations are done is given by the frequencies of visit counts of the actions,

$$\sigma_i^{final}(s, a_i) = \frac{n_{s,a_i}}{\sum_{b_i \in A_i(s)} n_{s,b_i}}.$$

Previous work [26] suggests first removing the samples caused by the exploration. This modification proved to be useful also in our experiments, so before computing the resulting final mixed strategy, we set

$$n_{s,a_i} \leftarrow \max\left(0, n_{s,a_i} - \frac{\gamma}{|A_i(s)|} \sum_{b_i \in A_i(s)} n_{s,b_i}\right). \tag{4}$$

3.3   Regret Matching

This variant applies regret matching [15] to the current estimated matrix game at each stage. Suppose iterations are numbered from $t \in \{1, 2, 3, \cdots\}$ and at each iteration and each decision node s there is a mixed strategy $\sigma_i^t(s)$ used by each player i for each node s in the tree, initially set to uniform random: $\sigma_i^0(s, a) = 1/|\mathcal{A}(s)|$. Each player i maintains a cumulative regret $r_s^i[a]$ for having played $\sigma_i^t(s)$ instead of $a \in \mathcal{A}_i(s)$. In addition, a table for the average strategy is maintained per player as well $\bar{\sigma}_s^i[a]$. The values in both tables are initially set to 0.

On iteration t, the selection policy (line 16 in Algorithm 1) first builds the player's current strategies from the cumulative regret. Define $x^+ = \max(x, 0)$,

$$\sigma_i^t(s, a) = \frac{r_s^i[a]}{R_{sum}^+} \text{ if } R_{sum}^+ > 0 \text{ oth. } \frac{1}{|\mathcal{A}_i(s)|}, \text{ where } R_{sum}^+ = \sum_{a \in \mathcal{A}_i(s)} r_s^{i,+}[a]. \quad (5)$$

The main idea is to adjust the strategy by assigning higher weight proportionally to actions based on the regret of having not taken them over the long-term. To ensure exploration, an γ-on-policy sampling procedure similar to Eq. 3 is used choosing action a with probability $\gamma/|\mathcal{A}(s)| + (1 - \gamma)\sigma_i^t(s, a)$.

The updates on line 14 and 19 add regret accumulated at the iteration to the regret tables r_s^i and the average strategy $\bar{\sigma}_s^i[a]$. Suppose joint action (a_1, a_2) is sampled from the selection policy and utility u_i is returned from the recursive call on line 18. Label the current child (i, j) estimate $\bar{X}_{s,i,j}$ and the $reward(i, j) = \bar{X}_{s,i,j}$ if $(i, j) \neq (a_1, a_2)$, or u_i otherwise. The updates to the regret are:

$$\forall a_1' \in \mathcal{A}_1(s), r_s^1[a_1'] \leftarrow r_s^1[a_1'] + (reward(a_1', a_2) - u_1),$$
$$\forall a_2' \in \mathcal{A}_2(s), r_s^2[a_2'] \leftarrow r_s^2[a_2'] + (reward(a_1, a_2') - u_2),$$

and average strategy updates for each player, $\bar{\sigma}_s^i[a] \leftarrow \bar{\sigma}_s^i[a] + \sigma_i^t(s, a)$.

The regret values $r_s^i[a_i]$ are maintained separately by each player, as in DUCT and depicted by Fig. 2. However, the updates and specifically the reward uses a value that is a function of the joint action space.

After the simulations, a move for the root s is chosen by sampling over the strategy obtained by normalizing the values in $\bar{\sigma}_s^i$.

3.4 Online Outcome Sampling

Online Outcome Sampling (OOS) is an MCTS adaptation of the outcome sampling MCCFR algorithm designed for offline equilibrium computation in imperfect information games [17]. Regret matching is applied but to a different type of regret, the sampled counterfactual regret. Counterfactual regret is a way to define individual regrets at s for not having played actions $a \in \mathcal{A}_i(s)$ weighted by the probability that the opponent played to reach s [28]. The sampled counterfactual regret is an unbiased estimate of the counterfactual regret.

In OOS, each simulation chooses a single exploration player i_{exp}, which alternates across simulations. Also, the probability of sampling to a state s due to the exploring player's selection policy, π, is maintained. These two parameters are added to the function in line 1 of Algorithm 1. Define $\sigma_i^t(s)$, regret and average strategy tables as in Subsect. 3.3. Regret matching (Eq. 5) is used to build the strategies, and the action selected for $i = i_{exp}$ is sampled with probability $p_{s,a_i} = \gamma/|\mathcal{A}(s)| + (1 - \gamma)\sigma_i^t(s, a_i)$. The other player j's action is selected with probability $p_{s,a_j} = \sigma_j^t(s, a_j)$. The recursive call on line 18 then sends down $\pi p_{s,a_i}$ as the new sample probability.

Upon return from the recursive call, the exploring player $i = i_{exp}$ first builds a table of expected values given their strategies $v_s^i[a]$. In outcome sampling, the values assigned to nodes that were not sampled are assigned a value of 0. This ensures that the estimate of the true counterfactual values remains unbiased. Due to the complexity of the implementation we omit this standard version of outcome sampling and refer interested readers to [18, Chapter 4]. Instead, we present a simpler optimized form inspired by Generalized MCCFR with probing [14] that seems to perform better in practice in our initial investigation. The idea is to set the value of the unsampled actions to their current estimated value. Define the child state $s_{\{a_i,a_j\}} = \mathcal{T}(s, a_i, a_j)$ if $(i,j) = (1,2)$ or $\mathcal{T}(s, a_j, a_i)$ otherwise. For the exploring player $i = i_{exp}$, for $a \in \mathcal{A}_i(s)$, the values are:

$$v_s^i[a] = \sum_{a' \in \mathcal{A}_j(s)} \sigma_j^t(s, a') X_{s,a'}^j \text{ where } X_{s,a'}^j = \begin{cases} u_i & \text{if } \{a, a'\} \text{ were selected} \\ \frac{X_{s'}}{n_{s'}} & \text{oth., where } s' = s_{\{a,a'\}} \end{cases}$$

The expected value of the current strategy for the exploring player $i = i_{exp}$ is then $v_{s,\sigma}^i = \sum_{i \in \mathcal{A}_i(s)} \sigma_i^t(s, a) v_s^i[a]$. The regrets are updated for $i = i_{exp}$ and average strategy for $j \neq i_{exp}$ as follows. For all $a_i \in \mathcal{A}_i(s)$ and all $a_j \in \mathcal{A}_j(s)$:

$$r_s^i[a_i] \leftarrow r_s^i[a_i] + \frac{1}{\pi} \left(v_s^i[a_i] - v_{s,\sigma}^i \right), \text{ and}$$

$$\bar{\sigma}_s^j[a_j] \leftarrow \bar{\sigma}_s^j[a_j] + \frac{1}{\pi} \sigma_j^t(s, a_j)$$

Finally, after all the simulations a move is chosen for player i by [21] selecting an action from the mixed strategy obtained by normalizing the values in $\bar{\sigma}_{s_{root}}^i$. We refer to this optimized version of OOS as OOS$^+$.

Since OOS is an application of outcome sampling to the subgame defined by the search tree, it converges to an equilibrium as the number of iterations at the same rate as outcome sampling MCCFR [18]. OOS$^+$ introduces bias and hence may not converge to an equilibrium strategy [14]. Approximate observed convergence rates are shown in Subsect. 4.3.

By way of example, consider Fig. 3. Suppose $i_{exp} = i = 1$, the trajectory sampled is the one depicted giving payoff u_1 to Player 1, and Player 1's sampled action sequence is a, c, e. Given this trajectory, Player 1's regret tables and Player 2's average strategies are updated at s_1, s_2, and s_3. Specifically at s_3, the matrix shown contains the reward estimates such that the top-left entry corresponds to $X_{s_3,e,f}/n_{s_3,e,f}$. The probability of sampling s_3 was $\pi = p_{s_1,a} \cdot p_{s_2,c}$. The values

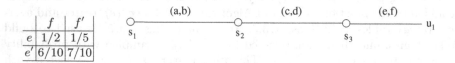

	f	f'
e	1/2	1/5
e'	6/10	7/10

Fig. 3. Example of online outcome sampling.

$v_{s_3}^i[e] = \sigma_j(s_3, f)u_1 + \sigma_j(s_3, f')/5,\ v_{s_3}^i[e'] = 6\sigma_j(s_3, f)/10 + 7\sigma_j(s_3, f')/10,$ and $v_{s,\sigma}^i = \sigma_i(s_3, e)v_{s_3}^i[e] + \sigma_i(s_3, e')v_{s_3}^i[e'].$

4 Empirical Evaluation

In this section we present and discuss the experiments performed to assess the practical behavior of the algorithms above.

4.1 Goofspiel

Goofspiel is a card game where each player gets N cards marked 1-N, and there is a central pile, shuffled and face down called the point-card deck (also 1-N). Every turn, the top card of this point card deck flips, it is called the *upcard*. Then, players choose a *bid* card from their hand and reveal it simultaneously. The player with the higher bid card obtains a number of points equal to the value of the upcard. The bid cards and upcard are then discarded and a new round starts. At the end of N rounds, the player with the highest number of points wins. If the number of points are tied, the game ends in a draw. The standard game of Goofspiel has $N = 13$, which has $(13!)^3 \approx 2.41 \cdot 10^{29}$ unique play sequences including chance events.

There are two ways to define the payoffs received at terminal states. Either the player with the highest points wins (payoffs $\{0, 0.5, 1\}$) or the payoff to the players is the difference in scores. We refer to the former as Win-Loss Goofspiel (WL-Goof(N)) and the latter as Point-Difference Goofspiel (PD-Goof(N)). A backward induction method to solve PD-Goof(N) was originally described in [22] and has recently been implemented and used to solve the game [21] for $N \leq 13$, therefore the optimal minimax value for each state is known. Our evaluation makes use of these in Subsect. 4.3. However, WL-Goof(N) is more common in the games and AI community [3,12,17,23].

Mixing between strategies is important in Goofspiel. Suppose a player does not mix and always bids with card n at s. An opponent can respond by playing card $n + 1$ if $n \neq 13$ and $n = 1$ otherwise. This counter-strategy results in collecting every point card except the one lost by the $n = 13$, leading to a victory by a margin of at least 78 points when $N = 13$. This remains true even if the point-card deck was fixed (removing all chance nodes). Nonetheless, the results presented below may differ in a game without chance nodes.

4.2 Head-to-Head Performance

To assess the individual performance of each algorithm, we run a round-robin tournament where each player plays against each other player $n = 10000$ times. This tournament is run using WL-Goof(13) and PD-Goof(13). Parameters are tuned manually by playing against a mix of the players. The metric used to measure performance in WL-Goof is win percentage with 0.5 win for a tie and in PD-Goof is the average number of points gained per game. Each player has

Table 1. Top: Win percentages for player 1 in WL-Goof(13), 95 % confidence interval widths ≤ 1 %. Bottom: Average points earned per game for player 1 in PD-Goof(13). 95 % confidence intervals widths ≤ 0.28. 10000 games per matchup. Draws considered half wins to each player to ensure the percentages sum to 100.

P1 \ P2	RND	DUCT(max)	DUCT(mix)	Exp3	OOS	OOS$^+$	Tuned Parm.
DUCT(max)	76.0						$C_i = 1.5$
DUCT(mix)	78.3	57.5					$C_i = 1.5$
Exp3	80.0	55.8	48.4				$\gamma = 0.2$
OOS	73.1	55.3	43.8	47.0			$\gamma = 0.5$
OOS$^+$	77.7	67.0	53.3	60.0	57.1		$\gamma = 0.55$
RM	80.9	63.3	53.2	57.2	58.3	50.4	$\gamma = 0.025$
DUCT(max)	12.92						$C_i = 150$
DUCT(mix)	11.88	0.91					$C_i = 150$
Exp3	13.18	4.15	3.17				$\gamma = 0.01$
OOS	10.69	3.33	0.82	−1.71			$\gamma = 0.5$
OOS$^+$	10.83	8.08	3.23	1.03	1.03		$\gamma = 0.4$
RM	12.94	6.60	3.41	1.12	1.05	0.17	$\gamma = 0.025$

1 s of search time and in our implementation each algorithm generally achieves well above 100000 simulations per second (see Table 2) using a single thread run on a 2.2 GHz AMD Opteron 6174. A uniform random strategy is used for the rollout policy. Ideally we are interested in the performance under different rollout policies, but we leave this as an interesting topic of future work.

The results are shown in Table 1. The RND player chooses a card to play uniformly at random. Of the MCTS variants, we notice that DUCT(max) had the worst performance, losing to every other algorithm in both games. In contrast, RM and OOS had the best performance, winning against every other algorithm in both games. RM's wins and gains against OOS$^+$ are not statistically significant, and OOS$^+$ seems to perform better against the other variants. This may mean that the reach probabilities and counterfactual values are important, even in the simultaneous move setting, the simplest form of imperfect information. However, in both games Exp3 appears to perform better than standard OOS. Also, some results differ between the two games, implying that their relative strength may vary. For example, in WL-Goof, RM wins 58.3 % vs. OOS and 53.2 % against DUCT(mix) and in PD-Goof wins only 1.05 points vs. OOS compared to 3.41 vs. DUCT(mix).

4.3   Exploitability and Convergence

After its simulations, each MCTS algorithm above recommends a play strategy for each state in the tree $\sigma_i(s)$. The exploitability of this strategy can be obtained by computing the amount it can lose against its worst-case opponent. Defined formally, $Ex(s, \sigma_i) = \max_{\sigma_j \in \Sigma_j}(V^*(s) - u_i(s, \sigma_i, \sigma_j))$, where $u_i(s, \sigma_i, \sigma_j)$ is the expected return of the subgame rooted at s when players use (σ_i, σ_j) and $V^*(s)$ is the optimal minimax value of state s. Zero exploitability means that σ_i is a Nash equilibrium strategy. Computing exact exploitability would require a strategy at

Table 2. Depth-limited exploitability at different depths and relative speeds in PD-Goof(11). 800 search samples per root state, 95 % confidence interval widths.

Algorithm	Mean Ex_2	Mean Ex_4	Mean simulations per second
DUCT(max)	7.43 ± 0.15	12.87 ± 0.13	124127 ± 286
DUCT(mix)	5.10 ± 0.05	7.96 ± 0.02	124227 ± 286
Exp3	5.77 ± 0.10	10.12 ± 0.08	125165 ± 61
OOS	$\mathbf{4.02 \pm 0.06}$	$\mathbf{7.92 \pm 0.04}$	186962 ± 361
OOS+	5.59 ± 0.09	9.30 ± 0.08	85940 ± 200
RM	5.56 ± 0.10	9.36 ± 0.07	138284 ± 249

every state in the game, which may not be well defined after short computation in the root. Therefore, we compute a depth-limited lower bound approximation to this value, which assumes optimal play after depth d:

$$Ex_d(s, \sigma_i) = \begin{cases} V^*(s) & \text{if } d = 0; \\ \sum_{s' \in \Delta_c(s)} \Delta_c(s, s') Ex_{d-1}(s', \sigma_i) & \text{if } s \in \mathcal{C}; \\ \max_{a_j \in \mathcal{A}_j(s)} \left\{ \sum_{a_i \in \mathcal{A}_i(s)} \sigma_i(s, a_i) Ex_{d-1}(T(s, a_i, a_j), \sigma_i) \right\} & \text{otherwise.} \end{cases}$$

It can be computed using a depth-limited expectimax search.

We assume that the player will not run additional simulations in the following moves and follow the strategy computed in the root until the end of the game. If this strategy is undefined at some point of the game, we assume selecting an arbitrary action. The mean exploitability values for depth $d \in \{2, 4\}$ over every initial upcard in PD-Goof(11), are shown in Table 2.

The results in Table 2 indicate that standard OOS, the only method known to converge to NE, produces the strategies with the lowest depth-limited exploitability for $d \in \{2, 4\}$. However, as seen in Subsect. 4.2 this does not necessarily lead to gains in performance, likely due to the restricted search time. Nonetheless, in a repeated play setting where opponents may adapt, less exploitable strategies are desirable. Each of the other algorithms produce less exploitable strategies than DUCT(max), which was expected in Goofspiel due to the importance of mixing. However, surprisingly, DUCT(mix) strategies are much less exploitable than expected. This begs the question of whether DUCT(mix) produces less exploitable strategies in Goofspiel, so in our next experiment we run the full best response to compute the full-game exploitability in smaller games of Goofspiel. Given the results below, we speculate that DUCT(mix) may be rotating among strategies in the support of an equilibrium strategy recommending a mixed strategy that coincidentally is less exploitable in PD-Goof(11) given the low search time. We do admit that more work is needed to clarify this point.

The next experiment evaluates how quickly the strategy computed by MCTS converges to a Nash equilibrium strategy in smaller game. We run MCTS with each of the selection strategies for 100000 iterations from the root and we computed the value of the full best response against this strategy after every 1000 iterations. The eight graphs in Fig. 4 represent the number of runs(out of

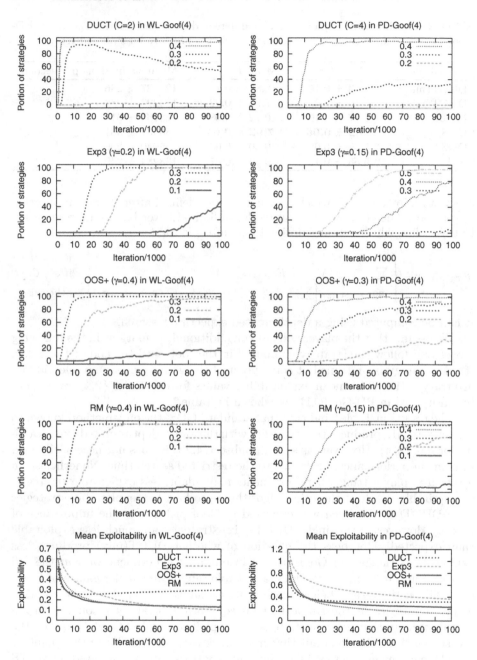

Fig. 4. The percentage of strategies produced by MCTS with exploitability lower than the given threshold after certain number of iterations in WL-Goof(4) (first four in left column), PD-Goof(4) (first four in right column) and mean exploitability for both Goofspiel versions (bottom two).

one hundred), in which the exploitability of the strategy was lower than the given threshold in PD/WL-Goof(4). For example with Exp3 in WL-Goof(4), the exploitability was always smaller than 0.3 after 30 thousand iterations and in 49 out of 100 runs, it was less than 0.1 after 100 thousand iterations. The last two graphs show the mean exploitability of the strategies. Consistently with the previous observations [25], the results show that DUCT does not converge to Nash equilibrium of the game. In fact, the exploitability of the produced strategy starts to increase after 20000 iterations. Exp3, OOS+, and RM strategies converge to the (at least good approximation of) Nash equilibrium strategy in this game. The computed strategies have low exploitability with increasing probability. In WL-Goof(4), OOS+ and RM converge much faster in the earlier iterations, but Exp3 converges more quickly and steadily with more iterations. In PD-Goof(4), RM clearly dominates the other strategies after 20000 iterations.

5   Conclusion and Future Work

In this paper, we compare six different selection strategies for MCTS in games with perfect information and simultaneous moves with respect to actual playing performance in a large game of Goofspiel and convergence to the Nash equilibrium in its smaller variant. The OOS strategy we introduced is the only one, which provably eventually converges to NE. After the whole tree is constructed, the updates behave exactly as in MCCFR, an offline equilibrium computation method with formal guarantees of convergence. The initial finite number of iterations, in which the strategy in some nodes was not updated cannot prevent the convergence. We believe OOS+, RM, and Exp3 also converge to Nash equilibria in this class of games, which we experimentally verify in the small Goofspiel games. We aim to provide the formal proofs and analysis of convergence rates in the future work.

The novel OOS+ and RM strategies have the quickest experimental convergence and performed best also in head-to-head matches. Both have beaten all the other strategies significantly and the performance difference in their mutual matches were insignificant.

In future work, we hope to apply some of these algorithms in the general game-playing and other simultaneous move games, such as Tron and Oshi-Zumo, and compare to existing algorithms such as SMAB and double-oracle methods to better assess their general performance. In addition, we are curious about the effect of different rollout policies on the behavior of each algorithm, the comparison to existing studies in UCT.

Acknowledgments. We would like to thank Laurent Bartholdi for sharing his code for solving Goofspiel. We would also like to thank Olivier Teytaud for advice in optimizing Exp3. This work is partially funded by the Netherlands Organisation for Scientific Research (NWO) in the framework of the project Go4Nature, grant number 612.000.938 and the Czech Science Foundation, grant no. P202/12/2054.

References

1. Auer, P., Cesa-Bianchi, N., Freund, Y., Schapire, R.E.: Gambling in a rigged casino: the adversarial multi-armed bandit problem. In: Proceedings of the 36th Annual Symposium on Foundations of Computer Science, pp. 322–331 (1995)
2. Auger, D.: Multiple tree for partially observable Monte-Carlo tree search. In: Di Chio, C., et al. (eds.) EvoApplications 2011, Part I. LNCS, vol. 6624, pp. 53–62. Springer, Heidelberg (2011)
3. Bosansky, B., Lisy, V., Cermak, J., Vitek, R., Pechoucek, M.: Using double-oracle method and serialized alpha-beta search for pruning in simultaneous moves games. In: Proceedings of the Twenty-Third International Joint Conference on Artificial Intelligence (IJCAI), pp. 48–54 (2013)
4. Browne, C.B., Powley, E., Whitehouse, D., Lucas, S.M., Cowling, P.I., Rohlfshagen, P., Tavener, S., Perez, D., Samothrakis, S., Colton, S.: A survey of Monte Carlo tree search methods. IEEE Trans. Comput. Intell. AI Games 4(1), 1–43 (2012)
5. Buro, M.: Solving the Oshi-Zumo game. In: Van Den Herik, H.J., Iida, H., Heinz, E.A. (eds.) Advances in Computer Games. IFIP, vol. 135, pp. 361–366. Springer, Heidelberg (2003)
6. Cazenave, T., Saffidine, A.: Score bounded Monte-Carlo tree search. In: van den Herik, H.J., Iida, H., Plaat, A. (eds.) CG 2010. LNCS, vol. 6515, pp. 93–104. Springer, Heidelberg (2011)
7. Chaslot, G.M.J.B., Winands, M.H.M., Uiterwijk, J.W.H.M., van den Herik, H.J., Bouzy, B.: Progressive strategies for Monte-Carlo tree search. New Math. Nat. Comput. 4(3), 343–357 (2008)
8. Couetoux, A., Hoock, J.-B., Sokolovska, N., Teytaud, O., Bonnard, N.: Continuous upper confidence trees. In: Coello, C.A.C. (ed.) LION 2011. LNCS, vol. 6683, pp. 433–445. Springer, Heidelberg (2011)
9. Coulom, R.: Efficient selectivity and backup operators in Monte-Carlo tree search. In: van den Herik, H.J., Ciancarini, P., Donkers, H.J. (eds.) CG 2006. LNCS, vol. 4630, pp. 72–83. Springer, Heidelberg (2007)
10. Cowling, P.I., Powley, E.J., Whitehouse, D.: Information set Monte Carlo tree search. IEEE Trans. Comput. Intell. AI Games 4(2), 120–143 (2012)
11. Finnsson, H.: Cadia-player: a general game playing agent. Master's thesis, Reykjavík University (2007)
12. Finnsson, H.: Simulation-based general game playing. Ph.D. thesis, Reykjavík University (2012)
13. Gelly, S., Kocsis, L., Schoenauer, M., Sebag, M., Silver, D., Szepesvári, C., Teytaud, O.: The grand challenge of computer go: Monte Carlo tree search and extensions. Commun. ACM 55(3), 106–113 (2012)
14. Gibson, R., Lanctot, M., Burch, N., Szafron, D., Bowling, M.: Generalized sampling and variance in counterfactual regret minimization. In: Proceedings of the Twenty-Sixth Conference on Artificial Intelligence (AAAI-12), pp. 1355–1361 (2012)
15. Hart, S., Mas-Colell, A.: A simple adaptive procedure leading to correlated equilibrium. Econometrica 68(5), 1127–1150 (2000)
16. Kocsis, L., Szepesvári, C.: Bandit based Monte-Carlo planning. In: Fürnkranz, J., Scheffer, T., Spiliopoulou, M. (eds.) ECML 2006. LNCS (LNAI), vol. 4212, pp. 282–293. Springer, Heidelberg (2006)
17. Lanctot, M., Waugh, K., Bowling, M., Zinkevich, M.: Sampling for regret minimization in extensive games. In: Advances in Neural Information Processing Systems (NIPS 2009), pp. 1078–1086 (2009)

18. Lanctot, M.: Monte Carlo sampling and regret minimization for equilibrium computation and decision-making in large extensive form games. Ph.D. thesis, Department of Computing Science, University of Alberta, Edmonton, Alberta, Canada (2013)
19. Littman, M.L.: Markov games as a framework for multi-agent reinforcement learning. In: Proceedings of the Eleventh International Conference on Machine Learning, pp. 157–163. Morgan Kaufmann (1994)
20. Perick, P., St-Pierre, D.L., Maes, F., Ernst, D.: Comparison of different selection strategies in Monte-Carlo tree search for the game of Tron. In: Proceedings of the IEEE Conference on Computational Intelligence and Games (CIG), pp. 242–249 (2012)
21. Rhoads, G.C., Bartholdi, L.: Computer solution to the game of pure strategy. Games 3(4), 150–156 (2012)
22. Ross, S.M.: Goofspiel – the game of pure strategy. J. Appl. Probab. 8(3), 621–625 (1971)
23. Saffidine, A., Finnsson, H., Buro, M.: Alpha-beta pruning for games with simultaneous moves. In: Proceedings of the Thirty-Second Conference on Artificial Intelligence (AAAI-12), pp. 556–562 (2012)
24. Samothrakis, S., Robles, D., Lucas, S.M.: A UCT agent for Tron: initial investigations. In: Proceedings of the 2010 IEEE Symposium on Computational Intelligence and Games (CIG), pp. 365–371 (2010)
25. Shafiei, M., Sturtevant, N.R., Schaeffer, J.: Comparing UCT versus CFR in simultaneous games. In: Proceeding of the IJCAI Workshop on General Game-Playing (GIGA), pp. 75–82 (2009)
26. Teytaud, O., Flory, S.: Upper confidence trees with short term partial information. In: Di Chio, C., et al. (eds.) EvoApplications 2011, Part I. LNCS, vol. 6624, pp. 153–162. Springer, Heidelberg (2011)
27. Winands, M.H.M., Björnsson, Y., Saito, J.-T.: Monte-Carlo tree search solver. In: van den Herik, H.J., Xu, X., Ma, Z., Winands, M.H.M. (eds.) CG 2008. LNCS, vol. 5131, pp. 25–36. Springer, Heidelberg (2008)
28. Zinkevich, M., Johanson, M., Bowling, M., Piccione, C.: Regret minimization in games with incomplete information. In: Advances in Neural Information Processing Systems 20 (NIPS 2007), pp. 905–912 (2008)

Decision Trees for Computer Go Features

Francois van Niekerk[✉] and Steve Kroon

Computer Science Division, Stellenbosch University, Stellenbosch, South Africa
francoisvn@ml.sun.ac.za, kroon@sun.ac.za

Abstract. Monte-Carlo Tree Search (MCTS) is currently the dominant algorithm in Computer Go. MCTS is an asymmetric tree search technique employing stochastic simulations to evaluate leaves and guide the search. Using features to further guide MCTS is a powerful approach to improving performance. In Computer Go, these features are typically comprised of a number of hand-crafted heuristics and a collection of patterns, with weights for these features usually trained using data from high-level Go games. This paper investigates the feasibility of using decision trees to generate features for Computer Go. Our experiments show that while this approach exhibits potential, our initial prototype is not as powerful as using traditional pattern features.

1 Introduction

In Computer Go, Monte-Carlo Tree Search (MCTS) is currently the dominant algorithm [1,2]. While the standard MCTS algorithm requires limited domain knowledge for a moderate level of strength [1], it has been shown that the inclusion of more domain knowledge can greatly increase the playing strength of Computer Go engines using MCTS [1,3,4]. One successful approach to incorporating such domain knowledge is using features [5]. This paper reports on a prototype implementation using decision trees as MCTS features in order to extract domain knowledge for Go.

After giving some background in Sect. 2, Sect. 3 describes our proposed method of using decision trees as features. Section 4 presents experimental results for the proposed approach.

2 Background

2.1 The Game of Go

Go is a combinatorial game played on a board consisting of a rectangular grid of intersections (a 19×19 grid is the most popular board size) [6]. Two players, black and white, alternate placing stones of their respective color on empty board intersections. Orthogonally contiguous stones of the same color form chains. If a chain of stones has zero adjacent empty intersections, also known as liberties, then the entire chain is removed from the board. The game ends after two successive passes — the winner is the player controlling the largest portion of the board.

T. Cazenave et al. (Eds.): CGW 2013, CCIS 408, pp. 44–56, 2014.
DOI: 10.1007/978-3-319-05428-5_4, © Springer International Publishing Switzerland 2014

2.2   Go Features for Monte-Carlo Tree Search

Monte-Carlo Tree Search (MCTS) is the current dominant algorithm in Computer Go and all the top engines make use of MCTS variants [1,2]. While hand-coded domain knowledge can quickly improve performance of MCTS engines, it is highly preferable to use automated methods of incorporating domain knowledge. One technique that successfully incorporates a large amount of domain knowledge in an automated manner is the use of Go features [5].

Go features are traditionally divided into pattern and tactical features [5]. Pattern features are simple encodings of the state of the surrounding board intersections. Tactical features encode simple domain knowledge not present in the pattern features, such as capturing a chain in atari (i.e. with only one remaining liberty). Each feature takes on one of a number of mutually exclusive levels. A comprehensive list of the tactical features used in this work is given in Table 1. Each potential move can then be described by a feature vector, with each vector component specifying which level a feature assumes for the candidate move. Patterns are typically represented by a single feature with many levels, with each level corresponding to a different pattern.

The intersections included in a pattern are typically all those within a certain distance from the center of the pattern. A popular distance measure used for large patterns in Go, and in this paper, is *circular distance* [5,7]: $\delta x + \delta y + \max(\delta x, \delta y)$, where $\delta x(\delta y)$ is the difference between the $x(y)$-coordinates of the pattern center and another intersection.

Feature levels for patterns should be invariant to changes in rotation, reflection, and whose turn it is to play. Invariance to player turns is usually achieved by swapping stone colors as necessary, while the invariance requirements for rotation and reflection are met by considering the eight combinations of rotation and reflection and using the pattern with the lowest hash value.

In order to make practical use of features, each level of each feature is assigned a trained weight, as discussed in Sect. 2.3. Feature weights corresponding to the levels in the potential move's feature vector are combined to form a compound weight for the move. These move weights can then be used in the MCTS tree to order moves for exploration, and in playouts for move selection.

2.3   The Generalized Bradley-Terry Model and Training Weights

In order to train weights for each feature level, features can be modeled using the generalized Bradley-Terry model for predicting the outcome of competitions between multiple teams of individuals [5]. In this model, the skill of each individual i is represented by a positive value γ_i, with a larger γ corresponding to a more skilled individual [5]. For training feature level weights, each individual represents a feature level and a team represents the feature vector for a potential move. The following example shows how the model predicts the outcome of a competition between teams of individuals [5]:

$$P(\text{1-2-3 wins against 2-4 and 1-5-6-7}) = \frac{\gamma_1\gamma_2\gamma_3}{\gamma_1\gamma_2\gamma_3 + \gamma_2\gamma_4 + \gamma_1\gamma_5\gamma_6\gamma_7}$$

A collection of competition results harvested from game records can be analyzed using this model — the resultant optimization problem (to determine the γ values, representing weights) can be approximately solved using minorization-maximization (MM), which has been shown to have good performance [5, 8].

Alternative techniques for training weights, not considered in this work, include Loopy Bayesian Ranking, Bayesian Approximation Ranking, Laplace$_q$ Marginal Propagation, and Simulation Balancing [8–10].

2.4   Graphs for Go

While simple Go patterns are useful, an alternative representation of the Go board is the Common Fate Graph (CFG) [11]. In the CFG of a Go board, each chain of stones and each empty intersection is represented by a single graph node. This causes certain functionally equivalent patterns to become equal. Due to computational concerns, their practical use in Computer Go has been limited — one notable concept arising from this representation is the *CFG distance* [2]. The decision tree approach in this work makes use of another graph representation for Go positions.

2.5   Decision Trees

Decision trees are tree structures with queries at internal nodes and values at leaves [12]. The queries evaluate the attributes of an input data point. In order to use a decision tree, the tree is descended, with the evaluated queries at internal nodes determining the descent path. The value stored at the resultant leaf is then typically used as a predicted outcome for the input.

Decision trees can be particularly sensitive to queries near the root of the tree. Decision forests, also known as random forests, can be used to construct a more robust model: this approach uses multiple decision trees that are grown from subsets of the input data to create an ensemble of decision trees. Such an ensemble of decision trees has been shown to yield more accurate classification than a single decision tree in many cases [13].

3   Decision Trees as Features

3.1   Overview

This section presents an approach to using decision trees as features for Go. An alternative way of viewing decision trees is that they partition the input space in a hierarchical fashion, and assign a predicted value to each element of the final partition, represented by the leaves. In our method, each query in a decision tree provides additional information about the surrounding board position — each node can be thought of as representing a pattern, with leaves representing the most complex patterns.

For this paper, we utilize a graph representation of the board: a *discovered graph* of the board area surrounding a candidate move is grown during each tree descent, such that the patterns represented by this graph at decision tree nodes grow in size and specificity as the tree is descended. If the discovered graph were grown to its maximum size and detail, it would yield the graph representation of the whole board.

A decision forest, an ensemble of such decision trees, is used to improve robustness. Each decision tree in the forest is treated as a separate feature with each leaf node corresponding to a unique feature level.

Section 3.2 presents the structure of these decision trees, by specifying our stone graph board representation and the form of the queries. In Sect. 3.3, a method for growing and training weights for the leaf nodes of such trees is described.

3.2 Structure

Queries in the decision tree are phrased in terms of a graph representation of the Go board and various representations are possible. In this work, we elected to use the following *stone graph* to represent the board position:[1]

- There is a node corresponding to each stone on the board and each of the four board sides.
- There is an edge between every pair of nodes.
- The weight of each edge is the Manhattan distance between the two stones (or the stone and board side) represented by the edge's end nodes on the board.
- Each node has, as applicable, attributes for the status (black, white or side), size (number of stones) and number of liberties[2] of its respective chain.

An additional node, that represents the empty intersection for the potential move under consideration, is then added to the stone graph to form the *augmented stone graph* (ASG). This node has edges to every other node in the ASG — these edges have weights allocated as in the stone graph. This node is labeled as node zero and referred to as the center. At the root of the decision tree the discovered graph contains only node zero. As the tree is descended, each query encountered either adds a node from the ASG to the discovered graph (as well as its edges to nodes in the discovered graph), or refines information about the attributes of a node or the weight of an edge already in the discovered graph.

Each decision tree query has multiple possible outcomes, one per child tree node. The queries were designed to be invariant to rotation and reflection as far as possible.

We specified three possible parametrized queries for expanding decision tree nodes — parameters are shown like [this]:

---

[1] This graph representation was chosen in the view that it may improve the opening of Oakfoam, the MCTS implementation being extended [14].

[2] A variation of pseudo-liberties [15] (where chains in atari have their number of pseudo-liberties set to one) was used to simplify implementation.

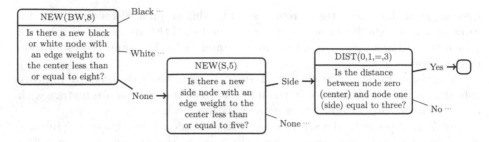

Fig. 1. A portion of an example decision tree showing a descent path. The leaf at the end of the descent path corresponds to a move on the fourth line with no stones within a Manhattan distance of eight.

NEW: Is there a new [**black? white? side?**][3] node with an edge weight to the center less than or equal to [**distance**]?
Look for a new node to add to the discovered graph from the ASG, and number the new node incrementally, if one is found. If multiple matching nodes in the ASG are found, attempt to select a unique node according to the rules found in Appendix A. Separate children are added to the decision tree for each allowed status, and none.

DIST: Is the edge weight between node [**x**] and node [**y**] [**less than|equal to**][4] [**val**]?
Query an edge of the discovered graph. Children are added to the decision tree for yes and no.

ATTR: Is the [**size|number of liberties**] of node [**x**] [**less than|equal to**] [**val**]?
Query a node of the discovered graph. Children are added to the decision tree for yes and no.

Figure 1 shows a portion of an example decision tree with a highlighted descent path. The leaf at the end of the descent path corresponds to a move on the fourth line with no stones within a Manhattan distance of eight. Note that node zero is the node representing the candidate move and, in this case, node one is the closest border. Also note that the distance between an intersection on the fourth line and the border is three.

3.3 Learning

Traditional decision trees attempt to partition the input space such that labels for points in the input space are homogeneous within partition elements. In our case, we do not have labeled points, so conventional decision tree training techniques are not applicable. Instead, we aim to construct our decision trees

---

[3] This parameter can be any combination of black, white and side, such as: black or side.

[4] [**x|y**] means either x or y.

such that the portion of input space corresponding to each of the final partition elements is roughly equal in size.

To achieve this, we choose queries that divide visits to children nodes roughly evenly. Statistics are gathered for candidate queries, and the query with the best split quality q is chosen when a certain number of descents to the respective node have occurred and the relevant quality is above a certain threshold. To divide tree descents evenly, we defined $q = 1 - 2|0.5 - s|$, where s is the proportion of visits to the last outcome for the candidate query.[5]

Once a decision tree has been grown, weights for the leaf nodes can be trained along with any other features using MM [5]. When a decision forest is used, each tree is independently grown and then the weights of all the trees are trained together (again with any other features). MM was chosen for training because it has been shown to have good performance, and there is a freely available tool that has been used for previous work, allowing us to verify our implementation for tactical and pattern features [5, 8].[6]

4   Experiments and Results

4.1   Overview

Our decision tree features will be used for move ordering, so their performance will first be tested on a move prediction task. We will then use the best configuration for a limited playing strength comparison.

Oakfoam [14] is an open source MCTS Go engine, used for the implementation and testing of these decision tree modifications. A collection of high-level 19×19 games played on KGS from 2001 to 2009 was used for training and testing. This data set is available from [16].

The following approach was used for extracting features and training their weights:

1. If enabled, harvest popular patterns from the collection. The number of games used is varied to adjust the number of patterns. Patterns with intersections within circular distances of 3–15 from their center, which occur at least 20 times in the considered games, are harvested.
2. If enabled, grow a decision forest by collecting statistics from games in the collection. A query is added to a node after at least 1000 descents to the node have occurred, and the quality is sufficient ($q \geq 0.4$ was chosen). The number of games used is varied to adjust the size of the trees.
3. Train weights for all the features using MM.

Only 10 % of the games' moves were used in order to sample from a large number of games. For decision forests, the 10 % of moves were independently sampled for each tree. Once the weights were trained, the appropriate test (move

---

[5] This is designed to deal with NEW queries that have more than two children.
[6] However, we later discovered that the MM tool was unable to deal with large training data sets for our tests.

prediction or strength comparison) was performed. More details on these tests follow in Sects. 4.2 and 4.3.

The sections that follow, the notation of x/y for decision forests is used to signify a decision forest comprising y trees with x leaves in total.

Table 1 lists the tactical features used in this work. The table also includes example weights for two configurations: one using tactical and pattern features, and another using tactical and decision tree features.

4.2 Move Prediction

For move prediction, features were used to compute move weights for all legal moves in a Go board position, and an ordering of the moves according to these weights was formed. The rank of the actual move played in this ordering was then used as a measure of move prediction accuracy. This process was repeated for every position in a collection of games. Each point on the resultant move prediction graphs show the proportion of positions where the actual move was within the top x ranked moves.

These move prediction tests were each performed on 100 19×19 games that are disjoint from the training data set. The 95 % confidence interval width, w.r.t. different testing data, for a single data point assuming 100 moves in each of the 100 games (typical for 19×19 games) is smaller than 0.02. These confidence intervals are therefore not shown on the graphs. Slight changes in the curves are observed for different training data sets, but more time would be needed to quantify this variance.

In the legends of the graphs that follow, tactical, pattern and decision tree features are indicated with T, P and DT respectively. The number of games used for training weights is indicated in square brackets; e.g.: "T + DT(10000/1) [1000]" indicates that the configuration used tactical and decision tree features, there was one decision tree with 10000 leaves, and that the weights were trained with 1000 games.

We first evaluated the effect of increasing the number of decision tree leaves, while keeping the number of trees fixed. This was done for a single decision tree and a decision forest with eight trees. The results are shown in Fig. 2. We found that move prediction accuracy improved as the number of leaves increased, but only up to a certain point.

We then investigated the impact of increasing the number of trees in the decision forest for a roughly fixed total number of leaves. We began with the strongest configuration from the previous series of tests: T + DT(17761/8) [4000]. The results are shown in Fig. 3. We found that increasing the decision forest from one to eight trees improved the move prediction accuracy. We also found that increasing the number of trees in the decision forest from eight to sixteen trees decreased the number of games we could use for training to 2000. This increase in decision forest size did not yield an improvement for move prediction, but it did require more processing time, so the previous configuration was kept for use in the next step.

Table 1. List of tactical features, with example weights from two configurations: γ^P for tactical and pattern features with 83644 patterns, and γ^{DT} for tactical and decision tree features with a 17761/8 decision forest. The weights for level zero of each feature are fixed at 1.0. When multiple feature levels are applicable, the highest level is selected.

Feature	Level	γ^P	γ^{DT}	Description
Pass	1	7.68	1.00	Pass after a normal move
	2	408.71	54.13	Pass after another pass
Capture	1	0.40	1.00	Capture a chain
	2	37.51	3.93	Capture a chain in a ladder
	3	2.21	8.71	Capture, preventing an extension
	4	3.04	11.80	Re-capture the last move
	5	14.59	42.03	Capture a chain adjacent to a chain in atari
	6	33.74	17.12	Capture a chain as above of 10 or more stones
Extension	1	5.06	10.07	Extend a chain in atari
	2	0.63	1.13	Extend a chain in a ladder
Self-atari	1	0.59	0.44	Self-atari of 5 or fewer stones
	2	0.21	0.16	Self-atari of more than 5 stones
Atari	1	1.92	1.84	Atari a chain
	2	0.84	0.60	Atari a chain and there is a ko
	3	2.03	2.19	Atari a chain in a ladder
Distance to border	1	0.43	0.84	
	2	1.12	1.16	
	3	1.51	1.16	
	4	1.20	1.13	
Circular distance to last move	2	9.18	13.36	
	3	6.44	7.75	
	4	3.57	4.37	
	5	3.27	3.79	
	...	...	...	
	10	1.53	1.68	
Circular distance to second-last move	2	1.41	1.67	
	3	1.54	1.77	
	4	1.23	1.14	
	...	...	...	
	10	1.08	1.10	
CFG distance to last move	1	2.98	2.63	
	2	3.38	2.96	

(continued)

Table 1. (continued)

Feature	Level	γ^P	γ^{DT}	Description
	3	3.42	3.26	
	4	2.13	1.97	
	...	...	...	
	10	1.06	1.02	
CFG distance	1	4.33	3.00	
to second-last move	2	3.39	2.51	
	3	2.50	1.70	
	4	2.08	1.66	
	...	...	...	
	10	1.16	1.08	

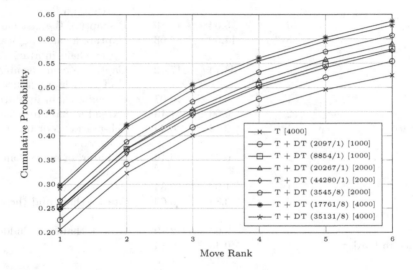

Fig. 2. Move prediction of tactical and decision tree features with different numbers of decision tree leaves.

Finally, we compared various combinations of tactical, pattern and decision tree features. The results are shown in Fig. 4. We found that tactical and decision tree features did not perform as well as tactical and pattern features, but that they showed a substantial improvement over tactical features alone. We also found that the inclusion of decision trees along with tactical and pattern features made no significant difference to move prediction accuracy.

4.3 Playing Strength

We used move prediction performance to select configurations for strength comparison tests — the configurations used in Fig. 4 were compared in terms of playing strength by playing a series of games against GNU Go [17]. All games

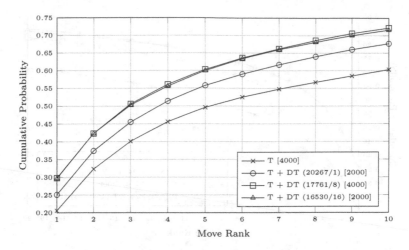

Fig. 3. Move prediction of tactical and decision tree features with different decision forest sizes.

Table 2. Comparison of playing strength of 10000 playouts per move vs GNU Go with various configurations. MP accuracy proportion of moves ranked best by the features used.

Tactical	Pattern	Decision forest	MP Accuracy (%)	Games	Winrate (%)
X	-	-	20.6	200	5.0
X	83644	-	35.3	300	49.0
X	-	17761/8	29.8	200	30.0
X	84237	16951/8	35.7	200	50.5

were played on 19×19 against GNU Go (version 3.8, level 10) with 7.5 komi and alternating colors starting on consecutive games. Playing strength was compared using 10000 playouts per move. This restriction was used because the aim was to investigate the feasibility of the decision tree features, and the prototype decision tree implementation was not optimized. For these tests, features were used for move selection during progressive widening in the MCTS tree [1,5]. Results of the strength comparison are shown in Table 2.

We found that the inclusion of decision tree features with tactical features resulted in a large increase in playing strength. We also found that the inclusion of decision tree features with tactical and pattern features did not result in a significant change to playing strength. These results are as expected from the move prediction results in Sect. 4.2.

5   Conclusions and Future Work

We have presented an approach using decision trees as features for extracting domain knowledge from game records for Computer Go. Our approach

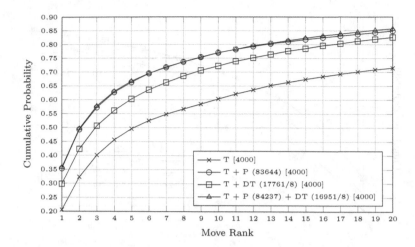

Fig. 4. Move prediction of the best configurations of each combination of pattern and/or decision tree features.

employs queries that refine knowledge of the current board position as the tree is descended. Our prototype implementation showed reasonable results in terms of move prediction and playing strength, although it did not perform as well as traditional pattern features. However, we believe there is significant potential for our method due to the general applicability of our method: many other board representations, query structures, and query selection criteria can be considered, and the general approach should be easily transferable to other domains.

One can specify tactical and pattern features as decision trees — from this perspective, our approach benefits from the structure of the tree being learned from training data, and not just the weights.

Our current work was not able to investigate larger decision trees, since the MM tool employed was not able to handle sufficient training data for these situations. To address this, we intend to explore other methods for training weights, such as $Laplace_q$ Marginal Propagation [9].

Acknowledgments. The first author would like to thank the MIH Media Lab at Stellenbosch University for the use of their facilities and support of the work presented here.

A   Multiple Decision Tree Descent Paths

It is possible that a NEW decision tree query may not be able to identify a unique node from the ASG to add to the discovered graph. In this situation, a sequence of conditions are considered, in an attempt to enforce uniqueness. Each condition will select the node(s) that best satisfy the condition and eliminate the others. These conditions are designed to enforce invariance to changes in rotation and reflection as far as possible. If the conditions are not able to identify a unique node, then each of the possibilities is considered.[7] The sequence of conditions used in this work is as follows:

- Select node(s) closest to the candidate move.
- Select black over white over side nodes.
- Select node(s) closest to nodes already in the discovered graph, in reverse order of discovery.
- Select node(s) with the most stones in its respective chain.
- Select node(s) with the most liberties around its respective chain.

Even though these conditions are not always able to find a unique node, empirical results showed that a single leaf node is reached in about 85 % of tree descents. It was therefore decided to only return one of these nodes, namely the left-most node in the tree. Investigation showed that this option made negligible difference to move prediction accuracy, while providing a large reduction in training time and an increase in the size of training data set that could be handled. This is due to the leaf nodes of each decision tree becoming mutually exclusive, allowing decision trees to be treated as single features.

B   Reproducibility

All source code used in this work is available in the codebase of Oakfoam, an open-source MCTS-based Computer Go player [14]. Version 0.1.3 was used for the work in this paper and is tagged in the code repository. Default parameters were used unless specified otherwise.

The MM tool of Rémi Coulom was used to train feature weights. This tool is available at: http://remi.coulom.free.fr/Amsterdam2007/.

References

1. Browne, C., Powley, E., Whitehouse, D., Lucas, S., Cowling, P.I., Rohlfshagen, P., Tavener, S., Perez, D., Samothrakis, S., Colton, S.: A survey of Monte Carlo tree search methods. IEEE Trans. Comput. Intell. Al Games **4**(1), 1–49 (2012)
2. Rimmel, A., Teytaud, O., Lee, C.-S., Yen, S.-J., Wang, M.-H., Tsai, S.-R.: Current frontiers in computer go. In: IEEE Symposium on Computational Intelligence and Al in Games, vol. 2, no. 4, pp. 229–238 (2010)
3. Gelly, S., Silver, D.: Combining online and offline knowledge in UCT. In: 24th International Conference on Machine Learning, pp. 273–280. ACM Press (2007)
4. Chaslot, G.M.J.-B., Chatriot, L., Fiter, C., Gelly, S., Perez, J., Rimmel, A., Teytaud, O.: Combining expert, offline, transient and online knowledge in Monte-Carlo exploration. IEEE Trans. Comput. Intell. Al Games (2008)
5. Coulom, R.: Computing elo ratings of move patterns in the game of go. ICGA J. **30**, 198–208 (2007)

---

[7] Note that this violates the conceptual view that the decision tree partitions the input space, since one position may ultimately correspond to multiple leaf nodes.

6. Baker, K.: The Way to Go. American Go Foundation (1986)
7. de Groot, F.: Moyo Go Studio. http://www.moyogo.com (2004)
8. Wistuba, M., Schaefers, L., Platzner, M.: Comparison of Bayesian move prediction systems for computer go. In: IEEE Conference on Computational Intelligence and Games, pp. 91–99, September 2012
9. Lew, L.: Modeling go game as a large decomposable decision process. Ph.D. thesis, Warsaw University (2011)
10. Huang, S.-C., Coulom, R., Lin, S.-S.: Monte-Carlo simulation balancing in practice. In: van den Herik, H., Iida, H., Plaat, A. (eds.) CG 2010. LNCS, vol. 6515, pp. 81–92. Springer, Heidelberg (2011)
11. Ralaivola, L., Wu, L., Baldi, P.: SVM and pattern-enriched common fate graphs for the game of go. In: European Symposium on Artificial, Neural Networks, pp. 485–490 (2005)
12. Russell, S., Norvig, P.: Artificial Intelligence: A Modern Approach, 3rd edn. Pearson, Englewood Cliffs (2010)
13. Breiman, L.: Random forests. Mach. Learn. 45(1), 5–32 (2001)
14. Oakfoam. http://oakfoam.com
15. House, J.: Groups, liberties, and such. http://go.computer.free.fr/go-computer/msg08075.html (2005)
16. Game records in SGF format. http://www.u-go.net/gamerecords/
17. GNU Go. http://www.gnu.org/software/gnugo/

UCT Enhancements in Chinese Checkers Using an Endgame Database

Max Roschke and Nathan R. Sturtevant[(✉)]

Department of Computer Science, University of Denver, Denver, CO, USA
max.roschke@gmail.com, sturtevant@cs.du.edu

Abstract. The UCT algorithm has gained popularity for use in AI for games, especially in board games. This paper assess the performance of UCT-based AIs and the effectiveness of augmenting them with a lookup table containing evaluations of games states in the game of Chinese Checkers. Our lookup table is only guaranteed to be correct during the endgame, but serves as an accurate heuristic throughout the game. Experiments show that using the lookup table only for its endgames is harmful, while using it for its heuristic values improves the quality of play. This work is performed on a board with 81 locations and 6 pieces, which is larger than previous work on lookup tables in Chinese Checkers. It is a precursor to using the 500 GB full-game single-agent data on the full-size board with 81 locations and 10 pieces.

1   Introduction

The UCT algorithm has recently proven to be a powerful tool for running simulations. Similar algorithms have been used to write powerful computer players for Go, a game which had long resisted other tactics. Its strength comes in part from its reliance on simulations, which approximate paths to the end of the game. After simulating to the end of the game, states are easily evaluated as a win or loss, so there is no explicit need for evaluation functions or expert knowledge. Even without these requirements, there are still many modifications that try to improve upon this model. A recent survey [2] lists over thirty potential enhancements across multiple domains, each with varying degrees of success.

Herein, we will test the effects of two enhancements to UCT in Chinese Checkers, each relying on a precomputed lookup table, which contains the distance of a single player's pieces to the goal state [13]. Towards the end of the game, this lookup table is effectively an endgame database and can be used to determine the winner and loser. It has already been demonstrated that opening books can improve the play of the UCT algorithm [1,3], so it seems reasonable to expect that endgame databases can also improve play. By knowing the endgame states, the playout length may be reduced, allowing for more playouts to run. Also, standard UCT playout policies may not follow the perfect endgame strategies. Thus, standard UCT may accept playouts where players make mistakes in the endgame. Using the lookup table to determine the exact value should eliminate

T. Cazenave et al. (Eds.): CGW 2013, CCIS 408, pp. 57–70, 2014.
DOI: 10.1007/978-3-319-05428-5_5, © Springer International Publishing Switzerland 2014

this possibility, making the simulations more accurate. Thus, we propose running simulations only until an endgame state is reached, rather than playing them out to completion.

Even during the mid-game, the lookup table may be used as an evaluation function. The information is not necessarily accurate, as it ignores the positions of the opponents pieces, but it may still favor advantageous board positions. These kinds of lookup tables have been used before in Chinese Checkers and have been found to produce a viable evaluation function [8,9,11]. The evaluation function becomes more accurate as the game progresses, as it eventually becomes an endgame database. This heuristic will be compared to a more common evaluation function that uses the average position of the pieces on the board. UCT will also be combined with the lookup table heuristic, to determine whether UCT estimations are a viable tactic for Chinese Checkers.

2   Background

2.1   Minimax Algorithm

The Minimax algorithm is a commonly-used technique for exploring the game tree of a two-player game. It creates a game tree of a certain depth, and then scores each leaf-state using an evaluation function. The evaluations are propagated up the tree with the player choosing the maximum value at his own nodes, and the opponent choosing the minimum value at its nodes. This explores all paths of that depth, and returns the best path for the player.

While simple, this algorithm provides a Nash equilibrium solution, allowing for a player to maximize his score for the given evaluation function. However, there are several drawbacks to this approach.

First, it has an exponential runtime. When searching a game with branching factor b to a depth of d, it has a runtime of $O(b^d)$. Using $\alpha\beta$-pruning, this can be reduced to $O(b^{d/2})$, but this is still gives a constraint on how deep the tree can be searched, especially in games with a large branching factor. There are other methods that attempt to improve on $\alpha\beta$-pruning, but we do not examine those here. Additionally, this approach does not scale well to multiplayer games. The $\max^n$ algorithm, the multiplayer equivalent, can only be pruned to $O(b^{(n-1)d/n})$ for n players [12].

Second, the result of the algorithm is only as accurate as the evaluation function itself. Evaluation functions are often inaccurate, as the middle stages of the game are ambiguous and difficult to rate. Any error in the evaluation function will become apparent in the results of the search.

2.2   UCT Algorithm

The UCT algorithm [5] relies on simulations to gather information about the game tree. It maintains a partial game tree in memory, and traverses it in four distinct stages: selection, expansion, simulation, and propagation.

First, an action is selected from the tree. At each node in the tree, an action is selected to maximize its UCB1 score, which is given by:

$$\overline{x_i} + C\sqrt{\frac{\ln(T)}{T_i}}$$

where $\overline{x_i}$ is the average payoff of an action, C is the exploration constant, T is the number of times the parent of the action has been played, and T_i is the number of times the action has been taken. The second part of the equation determines whether states are explored or exploited. The higher this second term, the less the score of the action depends on its average payoff, and the more it depends on the number of samples. A high C value encourages more exploration. This process is repeated until a leaf node of the tree is reached.

The leaf node may be expanded to add a new node to the tree, depending on the expansion policy of the tree. A common change is to only expand a node after it has been sampled a certain number of times [4]. This prevents the tree from growing rapidly, and tends to expand only nodes which have received better scores.

From this new node, a simulation is run to the end of the game. The simulation may be guided by a playout policy. In many games a random policy is acceptable, but in other games it is not. In fact, for some games, random playouts are completely unfeasible. For example, in Chinese Checkers, pieces may move both forwards and backwards, which means that the games may be infinite in length. Random playouts then would be too long and unrealistic to provide useful data about the game. For this reason, playout strategies are often imposed, for example, taking only forward moves and ignoring backward moves. If the playout policy matches usual player strategies, then this covers realistic play, and the simulations become more useful.

Finally, a win or loss is observed at the terminal game state, and that value is propagated up the tree. More information may be calculated at this terminal state to give an evaluation as well. For example, to emphasize shorter games, one may include the length of the simulation in its score. This value is then added to the total payout of each node on the path up the tree, updating its UCB1 score.

Many of these simulations are run, and then the best node is chosen from the tree. What constitutes the best node may be difficult to determine, as it should take into account both the sample rate and the average payout of that node.

Over time the game tree created by this algorithm approaches the actual minimax game tree which evaluates states based on wins, losses, or ties. When given infinite time and space to work with, it will eventually converge to that value [5]. However, this relies on all possible paths being traversed. Modifications to the tree, such as changing the playout and expansion policies, that cause some paths to be omitted from the tree eliminate this guarantee from a theoretical perspective.

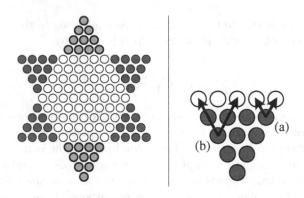

Fig. 1. A Chinese checkers board.

2.3 Chinese Checkers

Chinese checkers is a board game that can be played by two, three, four, or six players on an isometric board. Each player tries to move his pieces across the board, from his starting corner to the opposite corner. A player wins once all of his pieces have crossed the board, and are in the same configuration in which they started. The board is arranged into a hexagram when there are more than two players, and is simply a diamond when there are only two players. The piece counts may also vary; in smaller games, players have six pieces each, and in larger games, players have ten pieces each.

Pieces may move in two ways. They may move into adjacent empty spaces, or they may jump over an adjacent piece to a free space immediately opposite its original position (see Fig. 1 (right)). These jumps may be chained arbitrarily, so a piece may even move most of the way across the board on a single turn.

There is some ambiguity in the end of the game, as one player may leave pieces behind, preventing the opponent from filling that corner. However, to account for this case, we define a player to win once they have at least one piece across the board, and the tiles of that corner are all filled. Thus, if a player leaves pieces behind and the opponent fills all other spaces in that corner, the opponent wins. In this version of the game there can be no ties, as one player must reach the opposing side first. Games may also proceed indefinitely, as there is no restriction on the direction pieces may move. For simplicity, our experiments will be run on a nine-by-nine board with 81 possible locations for pieces – the same size as in the Fig. 1, but without the four blue corners – and each player will have only six pieces.

2.4 Endgame Databases

Endgame databases have proven effective in many other games. They contain all the necessary information to complete a game given a certain state. Chess programs make extensive use of these databases to improve play and many resources have been devoted to analyzing and generating these databases (see [14]). To date, all five-piece endgames have been calculated, giving the computer an immense amount of knowledge and sparing much computational time. These playouts can be especially complex, as many of them must take the fifty-move rule into account. While many databases do not specifically acknowledge the fifty-move rule in their returned solutions, the evaluation still gives the computer a glimpse of the probabilities of winning, losing, and drawing without doing any explicit calculation.

Endgame databases were also heavily used in the Checkers AI Chinook [10]. Move databases were extended to include all ending positions containing ten pieces or less, considerably increasing the accuracy of play.

Endgame databases have also been used before in Chinese Checkers and have been shown to improve the quality of play [8]. This has also been shown to aid UCT playouts as well [7], although their experiments were performed with smaller lookup tables than we will be using here.

3   Lookup Table

The lookup table is a simple table containing entries for all of the positions for a single player on the board [13]. Our experiments are run on a nine-by-nine board with each player having six pieces. This board has 81 positions, and is the board seen in Fig. 1 without the four blue corners. On this smaller board, there is an entry for each of the $\binom{81}{6} = 324,540,216$ positions. Each entry contains the minimum number of moves it would take that player to move all his pieces to the home area. This kind of database has been used before [7], although it was done on a seven-by-seven board, which contains much fewer positions.

Since this table only takes into account one player's pieces, it is not accurate when the players' pieces may interact. Opponent pieces may block the shortest path making the table value too low, or jumps offered by opponent pieces may offer a quicker path, making the table value too high. Table values are completely accurate once the pieces are separated. When there is no interference, the correct path is known, and players may complete the game with perfect play guided by lookups alone, so the lookup table may function as an endgame database.

While the lookup table is quite large, most of its entries are unused during the course of a normal game, so only a fraction of it needs to be loaded into memory. The entries are sorted by the furthest piece from the home area. All of the remaining pieces must be distributed after this starting piece, so there are $\binom{80-n}{5}$ positions for starting position n in general. As this back piece moves across the board, the number of potential configurations drops substantially (see Table 1). In most cases, this piece is not going to stay in the home area for long, as the pieces move quickest when kept in a group. This means that earlier, larger sections of the table can be omitted from memory, greatly reducing the memory requirements of the lookup table.

This is not a problem with the smaller data set, as the six-piece data can easily fit into memory. The ten-piece data set is much larger however, and cannot

Table 1. Lookup table size versus starting position

	Six pieces		Ten pieces	
Start position	# of positions	% of positions	# of positions	% of positions
1	324,540,216	100.000	1,878,392,407,320	100.000
5	237,093,780	73.055	1,096,993,404,430	58.401
10	156,238,908	48.142	536,211,932,256	28.546
15	99,795,696	30.750	247,994,680,648	13.202
20	61,474,519	18.942	107,518,933,731	5.724
25	36,288,252	11.181	43,183,019,880	2.299
30	20,358,520	6.273	15,820,024,220	0.842
35	10,737,573	3.309	5,178,066,751	0.276
40	5,245,786	1.616	1,471,442,973	0.078

easily be fit into memory. We have not run experiments on this larger data set yet, but some omission of data will be necessary to make its usage realistic.

4   Proposed Experiments

The experiments will be carried out on a nine-by-nine two player board. Each player will each have six pieces. This smaller board will lessen complexity and enable more trials to be run, but it is larger than boards used in previous experiments [7], so it will offer more information about the effects of board size on the table's effectiveness. Using this board configuration, we shall test two varieties of player. There will be two players using the $\alpha\beta$-pruning approach, and there will be three variations of the UCT algorithm. Each AI will be given a limit of 100,000 node expansions per move, allowing them equal access to resources.

4.1 $\alpha\beta$-Players

Each $\alpha\beta$ player will search to a depth of five ply using only non-backward moves. Backward moves are used much less often than other moves, and, in practice, led to a player that tried to block the opponent instead of moving his own pieces across the board. Removing the backwards moves also reduces the branching factor, leading to quicker play. These settings reached a balance of depth and speed, usually having the player respond in less than one second.

There will be two potential evaluation functions. The first uses the lookup table as a heuristic. The evaluation of a state will be the difference of the two players' values in the table. This will lead a player to block good opponent moves, while trying to move across the board as quickly as possible. The other function will be the difference in average position of the two players. Each player will check how many rows away from the home area their pieces are. This gives an approximation of how close the group is to winning. Again, using the difference should lead players to try and block each other, while moving quickly across the board, if possible.

Table 2. UCT parameters

Tree policy	Three variations: nodes in a tree may contain all moves, all non-backward moves, or all forward moves
Expansion policy	Nodes will only added to the tree once they have been visited a minimum number of times
Playout policy	Only forward moves are expanded for all playouts to reduce their length and approximate a reasonable strategy
Random move %	Some percentage of moves during the playouts are random, while the remaining moves are the farthest move – that which advances a piece the furthest number of rows
Weight of playout length	A small addition to the score which favors shorter wins or longer losses
C constant	The exploration versus exploitation value of the tree
Evaluation	Three variations: a win or loss value is returned once a simulation is completed, a win or loss value is returned once a simulation has reached a known endgame state, or an evaluation is returned once a simulation has run a set length

The lookup table may have an advantage over the simpler function, as it takes into account jumps and other factors that contribute to a piece's distance from the home area. Whether or not this information is truly more useful remains to be seen. These players will serve as a baseline, as their results do not depend on simulations. Without random simulations, they are guaranteed to give one solution for a given game state, so its results are less varied (Table 2).

4.2 UCT Players

Basic UCT. These players will be constructed with the standard UCT approach without any external knowledge. These players run simulations all the way to the end of the game, and then return a corresponding win or loss value. There are five variables which were tuned for this type of UCT player.

First, the expansion policy was varied. Nodes could only be placed into the tree after a certain number of samples had been run. There were three additional policies on the type of node that could be added to the tree. One policy added all nodes, another added only non-backward nodes, and the last added only forward moves. Experimentally, expanding only forward nodes gave the best results. Nodes were also not added to the tree until they had been sampled a minimum number of times.

Second, the playout policy was varied. All of these players only chose forward moves. However, there is much variation in the forward moves, so another variable was added. A set percentage of the time, the farthest move – one which took a piece the most rows toward its home state – was taken, while the remainder of moves was selected randomly. This attempts to model quick movement strategies, while allowing enough variation to give many sample points.

Third, the return value was augmented with the length of the simulation. Wins and losses accounted for most of the payout, but a small amount was varied based on the simulation length. Quick wins received a better evaluation than long wins, and long losses received a better evaluation than short losses. This steered the playouts to a better options, as quicker wins and longer losses are easier to exploit.

Finally, the C constant was tuned. This takes into account all of the other modifications and found the right amount of exploration versus exploitation for that combination of variables.

Tuning was done using a hill-climbing approach. Three players were created, each with a different category of playout policy, and the other four variables were tuned using the following procedure. All variables initially received a default value. A variable was selected and varied over a range of values near its current value. Six players, identical except for that variable, were created and all assume new values within that range. These six new players were pitted against the original (an equal number of times as first and second player), and the AI with the most victories was chosen as the new AI. The original remained if none of the new players defeated it more than fifty percent of the time. A single pass of tuning did this for each variable. Three passes were run on each policy, shrinking the range each time. The variables depend on each other, and each player was only tuned against variations of itself, so these tunings are in no way guaranteed to be optimal.

These tuned players gained the following configurations (some tuned parameters are omitted):

Name	Playout policy	Random move %	Expand threshold
$base_0$	Forward	17	18
$base_1$	Non-backward	14	18
$base_2$	All	22	20

Heuristic UCT Player. This version of the UCT player runs simulations to a fixed depth, and then evaluates them using the difference in distance, just like the $\alpha\beta$ lookup player. It was tuned using the same variables as the general UCT player – playout policy, random move percentage, expand threshold, and C constant– as well as two more: weight of the difference function and the playout depth. The difference function weight is just the linear weight of the difference function, and the playout depth is the number of moves playouts are run before the difference function is applied. All numeric constants were tuned with the same process used for the general UCT player.

Since this is the same evaluation function as the lookup-based $\alpha\beta$ player, this method will approximate the game tree value at that depth. This AI will evaluate the effectiveness of estimating that tree's value.

The technique of stopping a UCT simulation early has been used before in the game of Amazons [6]. Their AI also did the best after a certain number of random moves had been played – the same tactic that we shall use here.

The tuned players gained the following configurations:

Name	Playout policy	Random %	Expand threshold	Playout depth
$heur_0$	Forward	43	32	13
$heur_1$	Non-backward	55	20	13
$heur_2$	All	32	27	14

Endgame UCT Player. This UCT Player runs simulations until the players are separated. Separation is determined using the centerline of the board as a divider. Once the player and their opponent's pieces are on opposite sides of the centerline, the pieces are considered separated. This is not entirely accurate, as it is still possible for a piece to jump to the centerline and then interact with opposing pieces. However, the likelihood of this is small, and it is even less likely that this would benefit or hinder either player.

Once separated, the winner is declared based on each player's distance from his respective goal. All other variables remained the same as the general UCT player.

Name	Moves in tree	Random %	Expand threshold
end_0	Forward	17	18
end_1	Non-backward	6	2
end_2	All	21	23

5   Experiment Results and Analysis

5.1   Depth-Based Trials

Table 3 shows the results of the best players in each category. While three versions were created in each category, these were the strongest. The player on the left played as first player, while the player on top played as second player. The percentage shown is the winning percentage of the first player. All results are out of 100 trials, except for the $\alpha\beta$ results, which are not listed, as there is no randomness in their algorithms, hence, no variation. The UCT algorithms were given 100,000 node expansions per move. The best tree expansion policy turned out to use only forward moves. In practice, when the players were allowed to use all moves, they tended to play overly defensively, and attempted to block the opponent more than they tried to cross the board. This became especially true when they started to lose, as the evaluation function gave better results for blocking the opponent's advances.

There appears to be a slight bias towards the first player. The general trials showed advantages of approximately 5 % more wins for the first player.

The general UCT player tends to do better than the average-based $\alpha\beta$ player, taking an average amount of second player wins (after accounting for the first player advantage), and winning many more first player rounds. It fails to beat

Table 3. Results for the best players using 100 trials

Player one wins (first player left, second player top)	$\alpha\beta$	$\alpha\beta$-lookup	$base_0$	$heur_0$	end_0
$\alpha\beta$	–	–	54.0%	18.0%	67.0%
$\alpha\beta$-lookup	–	–	75.0%	36.0%	88.0%
$base_0$	83.0%	65.0%	56.0%	5.0%	62.0%
$heur_0$	96.0%	87.0%	96.0%	67.0%	97.0%
end_0	72.0%	27.0%	43.0%	5.0%	49.0%

the $\alpha\beta$ player that uses the lookup table, however, indicating that the lookup table serves as a decent evaluation function throughout the game.

Further, the lookup table heuristic appears much more accurate than the average distance metric based on the relative performances of the $\alpha\beta$ players. The $\alpha\beta$ player using the lookup table won an additional 18% of the rounds as first player than the $\alpha\beta$ player without that data. It was also able to better defend itself as second player, winning at least 9% more of the overall rounds.

Of the two enhancements to UCT, using the lookup table as a heuristic appears much more effective than using it solely to calculate endgames. While the additional of heuristic values resulted in a stronger player, the addition of endgames lowered the quality of play.

5.2 Sample Based Trials

For this experiment (see Table 4), players were only allowed to complete a certain number of playouts before they made a move. This would remove the benefits of shorter playouts of the heuristic player and the endgame player, as there are a limited number of playouts regardless of depth.

Versus the plain UCT player, the heuristic player's performance suffered. As second player, it lost several times the games that it did in the node expansion experiment. It also did slightly worse as the first player. However, these results do not seem to vary consistently with the number of playouts. Increasing the number of playouts allowed per turn did not give an advantage to either player.

Table 4. Trials with limited number of playouts (200 trials)

Player one win rates						
		Number of playouts per turn				
p1	p2	1,000	2,000	4,000	8,000	16,000
$base_0$	$heur_0$	13.0%	12.5%	12.5%	17.0%	11.5%
$heur_0$	$base_0$	88.5%	92.5%	94.5%	90.5%	94.0%
$base_0$	end_3	63.0%	61.5%	74.0%	70.0%	80.5%
end_3	$base_0$	49.5%	46.0%	40.5%	37.0%	27.5%
$heur_0$	end_3	97.0%	97.5%	100.0%	98.5%	99.5%
end_3	$heur_0$	6.5%	4.0%	3.0%	1.5%	1.5%

The plain UCT Player benefitted from more playouts when put against the endgame player. As the number of playouts per turn increased, so did the wins of the plain UCT player as both first and second player.

The heuristic player also did better against the endgame player when allowed more playouts per turn. As first player, the heuristic model won almost all of the time, and as second player it won almost all matches when allowed at least 4,000 playouts per turn.

Overall, both the heuristic and the endgame players suffered some performance penalties. The basic UCT player improved its performance as both the first and second player compared to the two models that shortened playouts. However, the heuristic model remained as the clear winner between these three strategies.

5.3   Time Based Trials

Next, we considered giving an equal amount of time to each player. This would show more of the strengths and weaknesses of each approach. The plain UCT player has no cost for lookups, and never needs to check if a state is in memory, but also then must play each playout game to completion. The heuristic player only plays to a static depth before looking up the end state in memory, which should take little time overall. The endgame player must play out a game until each player is in a state that is in memory. This likely will take the longest time, as it has to check its states most often. This will then vary the number of playouts each player can run in a turn, giving an advantage to the faster players (Table 5).

The heuristic player remained strong versus the plain UCT player under time trials, while the endgame player did not. The heuristic player won most of its matches, only once having its win rate drop below 90 %. This did not seem to vary on the overall time, as the rates remained close as time increased per turn.

Table 5. Trials with limited time per turn

| | | Player one win rates | | | |
| | | Time per turn | | | |
p1	p2	1 s	2 s	4 s	8 s
$base_0$	$heur_0$	10.6 %	8.0 %	7.0 %	9.0 %
$heur_0$	$base_0$	95.0 %	93.5 %	97.0 %	97.0 %
$base_0$	end_3	55.6 %	62.5 %	56.5 %	59.0 %
end_3	$base_0$	51.9 %	49.0 %	57.5 %	54.0 %
$heur_0$	end_3	98.8 %	99.0 %	96.0 %	94.0 %
end_3	$heur_0$	8.1 %	4.0 %	1.5 %	3.0 %

1 s results from 160 trials
2 and 4 s results from 200 trials
8 s results from 100 trials

The endgame player was able to match the strength of the plain UCT player almost evenly. Each player usually won between 50 and 60 percent of matches when playing as first player. This matches previous indications of a first player bias, so these players seem evenly matched when given equal amounts of time to think.

The endgame player did not play well versus the heuristic player and lost most of the matches it played. This seemed to vary little with time. Although it did the best during the 1 s trials as first player, this could be due to the granularity of the timer used. It also seemed to fare better as the time was increased as second player, as it was able to win six percent of its matches with more time.

When given equal amounts of time, the plain UCT was able to perform 1.5 times as many node expansions as the heuristic player, and twice as many as the endgame player. When playing each other, the endgame and heuristic players expanded roughly the same number of nodes.

6   Conclusions and Further Work

There are several conclusions to be drawn from these results. First, it would seem that the lookup table serves as a good heuristic throughout the game. Not only was the $\alpha\beta$ search able to challenge the UCT players effectively, but the UCT player using this heuristic was able to win more than 85 % of its first player games, and more than 60 % of its second player games. This leads to the second point, that using the UCT algorithm to approximate the game tree at a certain depth gives useful results. Since both the UCT algorithm and this $\alpha\beta$ were using the same heuristic, it would seem that the approximation of the heuristic at a depth of fourteen proved more useful than the exact value of that heuristic at depth five.

While the endgame databases caused performance to suffer here, it should not be taken as a general trend. It outperformed the average-based $\alpha\beta$ player, but fell short of defeating the lookup-based $\alpha\beta$ player. This is only based on 100,000 node expansions, however, which is less than one second of calculation per move. Additionally, the tuning procedure was not guaranteed to be optimal. Given more resources, the performance of the endgame player will likely improve.

In general, the heuristic player was shown to give the best results in both time-dependent and time-independent trials. It would seem that the lookup table provides useful, general information about the state of the game. In terms of the larger lookup table, however, this may not be true. In this case, with a lookup table that can completely fit into memory, it is feasible to lookup any state of the board. This strategy requires that option, for it always plays a fixed number of moves ahead. This is less easily accomplished with a larger table, so the performance of this player will likely suffer the most from increases to the lookup table's size.

More work can be done on expanding these results. These results can be scaled up by giving the players more time to make each move. This will give the algorithms more time to converge to a good move, and it will show the cost of each approach. Time trials show that the plain UCT player is much faster than either the heuristic player or the endgame player, and this advantage will only become greater as the size of the lookup table increases. These trials still contain reasonably small tables (approximately 350 Mb at largest). Once the tables can no longer fit into memory, these lookups will be even longer.

The lookup table size will also be scaled up. We have the ten-piece data set, which presents its own challenges. While these players were able to freely query the lookup table for any state, players querying the ten-piece data set will need to confront the massive size of that data set. The effects of loading only portions of the database will be examined, as well as the effects on time. A larger lookup table means that the queries will likely take longer, further reducing the number of trials these players will be able to run.

References

1. Audouard, P., Chaslot, G., Hoock, J.-B., Perez, J., Rimmel, A., Teytaud, O.: Grid coevolution for adaptive simulations: application to the building of opening books in the game of Go. In: Giacobini, M., Brabazon, A., Cagnoni, S., Di Caro, G.A., Ekárt, A., Esparcia-Alcázar, A.I., Farooq, M., Fink, A., Machado, P. (eds.) EvoWorkshops 2009. LNCS, vol. 5484, pp. 323–332. Springer, Heidelberg (2009)
2. Browne, C., Powley, E.J., Whitehouse, D., Lucas, S.M., Cowling, P.I., Rohlfshagen, P., Tavener, S., Perez, D., Samothrakis, S., Colton, S.: A survey of monte carlo tree search methods. IEEE Trans. Comput. Intell. AI Games 4(1), 1–43 (2012)
3. Chaslot, G.M.J.-B., Hoock, J.-B., Perez, J., Rimmel, A., Teytaud, O., Winands, M.H.M.: Meta monte-carlo tree search for automatic opening book generation. In: Proceedings of the 21st International Joint Conference on Artificial Intelligence, Pasadena, California, 2009, pp. 7–12 (2009)
4. Coulom, R.: Efficient selectivity and backup operators in Monte-Carlo tree search. In: van den Herik, H.J., Ciancarini, P., Donkers, H.J. (eds.) CG 2006. LNCS, vol. 4630, pp. 72–83. Springer, Heidelberg (2007)
5. Kocsis, L., Szepesvári, C.: Bandit based Monte-Carlo planning. In: Fürnkranz, J., Scheffer, T., Spiliopoulou, M. (eds.) ECML 2006. LNCS (LNAI), vol. 4212, pp. 282–293. Springer, Heidelberg (2006)
6. Lorentz, R.J.: Amazons discover Monte-Carlo. In: van den Herik, H.J., Xu, X., Ma, Z., Winands, M.H.M. (eds.) CG 2008. LNCS, vol. 5131, pp. 13–24. Springer, Heidelberg (2008)
7. Nijssen, J.A.M., Winands, M.H.M.: Playout search for Monte-Carlo tree search in multi-player games. In: van den Herik, H.J., Plaat, A. (eds.) ACG 2011. LNCS, vol. 7168, pp. 72–83. Springer, Heidelberg (2012)
8. Samadi, M., Schaeffer, J., Torabi Asr, F., Samar, M., Azimifar, Z.: Using abstraction in two-player games. In: ECAI, pp. 545–549 (2008)
9. Schadd, M.P.D., Winands, M.H.M.: Best reply search for multiplayer games. IEEE Trans. Comput. Intell. AI Games 3(1), 57–66 (2011)
10. Schaeffer, J., Björnsson, Y., Burch, N., Lake, R., Lu, P., Sutphen, S.: Building the checkers 10-piece endgame databases. In: van den Herik, H.J., Iida, H., Heinz, E.A. (eds.) Advances in Computer Games 10, pp. 193–210. Springer, New York (2003)

11. Sturtevant, N.R.: A comparison of algorithms for multi-player games. In: Schaeffer, J., Müller, M., Björnsson, Y. (eds.) CG 2002. LNCS, vol. 2883, pp. 108–122. Springer, Heidelberg (2003)
12. Sturtevant, N.R.: Last-branch and speculative pruning algorithms for max^n. In: Gottlob, G., Walsh, T. (eds.) IJCAI, pp. 669–678. Morgan Kaufmann (2003)
13. Sturtevant, N.R., Rutherford, M.J.: Minimizing writes in parallel external memory search. In: International Joint Conference on Artificial Intelligence (IJCAI), pp. 666–673 (2013)
14. Thompson, K.: Retrograde analysis of certain endgames. ICCA J. **9**(3), 131–139 (1986)

Automated Generation of New Concepts from General Game Playing

Yuichiro Sato[1](✉) and Tristan Cazenave[2]

[1] Japan Advanced Institute of Science and Technology, Nomi, Japan
sato.yuichiro@jaist.ac.jp
[2] Université Paris-Dauphine, Paris, France
cazenave@lamsade.dauphine.fr

Abstract. In this paper, we propose algorithms to extract explicit concepts from general games and these concepts are useful to understand semantics of games using General Game Playing as a research domain. General Game Playing is a research domain to invent game players which are able to play general games without any human intervention. There are many approaches to General Game Playing, for example, UCT, Neural Network, and Simulation-based approaches. Successful knowledge acquisition is reported in these approaches. However, generated knowledge is not explicit in conventional methods. We extract explicit concepts from heuristic functions obtained using a simulation based approach. Concepts to understand the semantics of Tic-tac-toe are generated by our approach. These concepts are also available to understand the semantics of Connect Four. We conclude that our approach is applicable to general games and is able to extract explicit concepts which are able to be understood by humans.

1 Introduction

An intelligent system is able to adapt itself to its environment. To invent artificial intelligence, it is a good strategy to make a program which learns knowledge from the environment. We can use our living world itself as the environment for a system, e.g., Natural Language Processing. In this study, we focus on artificial environments, i.e., games. A game has concrete rules, and is easy to simulate and evaluate without any human intervention. We tried to discover new concepts from experience in this artificial environment. We use General Game Playing (GGP) as a research domain. GGP is a research domain to invent game players which are able to play general games.

There are many General Game Players. J. Méhat et al. developed a UCT based player [8], and D. Michulke et al. developed a machine learning based player [9]. Also, simulation and knowledge based approaches are studied. T. Kaneko et al. developed a successful method to learn logical features using a Boolean network approach [5]. P. Skowronski et al. extracted features for selective search extensions [12]. H. Finnsson et al. also extracted knowledge for general games to improve search efficiency of their player [1,3]. However, generated

T. Cazenave et al. (Eds.): CGW 2013, CCIS 408, pp. 71–80, 2014.
DOI: 10.1007/978-3-319-05428-5_6, © Springer International Publishing Switzerland 2014

knowledge is not explicit in these conventional research. In this study, we propose the generation of new concepts which are explicit enough to be understood by humans.

2   Method

We made our General Game Player using ECLiPSe Prolog and Java. It reads games expressed in the Game Description Language (GDL) [7] through a parser [11] into a Prolog engine, then the engine is called from Java through a Java-Prolog interface to simulate a game.

We automatically produced heuristics for the game by statistical analysis of simulation results. GDL is convertible to first-order predicate logic, therefore we can write GDL in Prolog [8]. Also, we can write positions of games as Prolog like facts. Thus, we made heuristics out of a set of Prolog rules. For each rule, the body is a subset of a game position, and the argument of head is the evaluation value of the position.

$$evaluation(value) : -a\_subset\_of\_position\_of\_game. \tag{1}$$

We used Tic-tac-toe and Connect Four as subject games. In Tic-tac-toe, x player and o player try to make a straight line on a 3×3 two-dimensional board using his/her mark. In Connect Four, white player and red player also try to make a straight line with one's color, but the board size is 7×6. Additionally, it has gravity, so the players need to drop the tokens of their color from the top and pile them up. Therefore, players need to play Connect Four using a different strategy to Tic-tac-toe.

Even though the game rules are different, the representation of the board is shared by both games. In both games, a board is represented by a set of cell terms with arity 3, two arguments are for the coordinate and one is for the mark or color on the cell. This situation is convenient for our purpose.

3   Automated Generation of Heuristic Functions from Simulations

We tried automated generation of heuristic functions from random simulations of Tic-tac-toe and Connect Four. J. Clune successfully generated heuristic functions for GGP [2]. M. Kirci et al. successfully extracted winning positions of general games from playouts [6]. We statistically evaluated positions.

We simulated Tic-tac-toe games till we got 10,000 playouts with each player as the winner. Then, we counted up what kind of subset of position is included in playouts and calculated the frequency to appear for each player. Finally, we picked the top 10 % of frequent subsets and made Prolog rules which have the frequency as its evaluation value as written in Algorithm 1. We cut off Prolog rules in the heuristic functions which have greater body size than a specific size.

We made three heuristic functions by using three different cut off sizes, 1, 2 and 3.

The following rules were included in generated heuristic functions.

$$evaluation(0.238...) : -cell(3,1,o), cell(2,2,o). \tag{2}$$
$$evaluation(0.237...) : -cell(3,3,o), cell(2,2,o), cell(1,3,x). \tag{3}$$

These heuristics are appropriate for Tic-tac-toe. An evaluation value of a position is a sum of evaluation values of heuristic functions which match to the position. We generated heuristic functions in the same way for Connect Four by 1000 simulations for each player. For Connect Four, we used a cut off size of 1 and 2. We omitted cut off size 3 to reduce simulation time.

We evaluated the performance of each heuristic function by simulation. In the simulation, a 1-depth alpha-beta search player with each heuristic function played against both a random player and a 1-depth alpha-beta search player without heuristics. The 1-depth alpha-beta search player chooses a winning move when it is found by 1-depth search. Otherwise, the player chooses a random move. We did 10,000 simulations for Tic-tac-toe, 1000 simulations for Connect Four. Against a random player, for both games, winning ratios tend to improve when the cut off size gets greater, as can be seen in Table 1. If the cut off size is 0, it means that the player has no heuristic function. The same tendency was seen against an alpha-beta search player in Table 2. These results suggest that this algorithm successfully extracted features of games properly and encoded them as heuristic functions.

Algorithm 1 makeStatisticalHeuristics($playouts$)

$M \Leftarrow$ Hash Map
for all playout p in $playouts$ **do**
   $S \Leftarrow$ getSubset(p)
   for all subset s in S **do**
      if M contains s **then**
         increment counter for s
      else
         create hash for s and set the counter as 1
      end if
   end for
end for
for all m in M **do**
   $v \Leftarrow$ counter for m / size of $playouts$
   add Prolog rule type heuristic, "evaluation(v):-m." into H
end for
$H \Leftarrow$ pick up rules which have top 10% of its evaluation value from H
return H

Table 1. Evaluation of heuristic functions for Tic-tac-toe and Connect Four against a random player.

game	player	cut off size			
		0	1	2	3
game	player	win(%)/lose(%)/draw(%)			
Tic-tac	x	80.73/12.32/6.95	93.38/4.53/2.09	90.17/7.45/2.38	96.49/2.76/0.75
-toe	o	50.57/40.69/8.74	65.64/27.50/6.86	68.10/28.11/3.79	73.65/24.77/1.58
Connect	white	81.4/18.6/0	84.4/15.6/0	90.2/9.8/0	-
Four	red	71.3/28.6/0.1	70.4/29.6/0	77.4/22.6/0	-

Table 2. Evaluation of heuristic functions for Tic-tac-toe and Connect Four against a 1-depth alpha-beta search player.

game	player	cut off size			
		0	1	2	3
game	player	win(%)/lose(%)/draw(%)			
Tic-tac-toe	x	67.98/27.51/4.51	85.81/13.57/0.62	74.53/25.47/0	91.42/8.58/0
	o	27.00/68.71/4.29	41.78/55.40/2.82	41.95/57.87/0.18	50.42/49.58/0
Connect	white	57.4/42.6/0	62.2/37.8/0	79.7/20.3/0	-
Four	red	40.1/59.9/0	40.4/59.6/0	54.4/45.6/0	-

4 Automated Generation of New Concepts for Games from Heuristic Functions

We consider that heuristic functions include essential concepts about games. We tried to extract them as explicit new concepts. This is the Predicate Invention, one of the research areas of Inductive Logic Programming [4].

First, for all Prolog rules in each heuristic function, we made pairs of terms included in its body. Then we replaced arguments with variables in the pairs if an argument in one of the terms in the pair relates to the corresponding argument in the other term. If an argument was a number, the argument was replaced by a new variable and the other was replaced by the sum of the variable and the difference between the two arguments. If the arguments were the same strings, we replaced them with a new variable. We introduced variables into original terms in this way. After removing duplicates, finally we got explicit new concepts from Prolog like heuristic functions, as written in Algorithm 2.

We extracted new concepts from heuristic functions for Tic-tac-toe generated in Sect. 3. Typical concepts are as follows.

$$concept1(X_0, X_1, X_2) : -cell(X_0, X_1, X_2), cell(X_0, X_1 + 1, X_2). \quad (4)$$

$$concept11(X_0, X_1, X_2) : -cell(X_0, X_1, X_2), cell(X_0 + 2, X_1 + 2, X_2). \quad (5)$$

$$concept20(X_0, X_1) : -cell(X_0, X_1, x), cell(X_0 + 2, X_1 + 2, o). \quad (6)$$

We are able to interpret these concepts as human language. Equation 4 means "a cell and its right cell are marked by the same symbol". Equation 5 means "a cell and its lower right cell are marked by the same symbol". Equation 6 means "a cell is marked by x and its lower right cell is marked by o". These are natural concepts for humans to play Tic-tac-toe. Concepts which have a variable as the role argument are general concepts which are available for both Tic-tac-toe and Connect Four. Concepts which do not have a variable as the role argument are specialized for Tic-tac-toe and not available for Connect Four because role symbols are different between Tic-tac-toe and Connect Four.

Algorithm 2 generateNewConcept(*prolog_rules*)

---

  for all rule r in *prolog_rules* **do**
    $P \Leftarrow$ all pairs of terms in the body of r
    for all pair (p_1, p_2) in P **do**
      for $i = 0$ to arity of p_1 **do**
        if i-th argument of p_1, a_i and i-th argument of p_2, b_i are instances of the
        same class **then**
          if a_i is an instance of number **then**
            replace a_i to a new variable and b_i to sum of the variable and $b_i - a_i$
          else if a_i equals to b_i **then**
            replace a_i and b_i to a new variable
          end if
        end if
      end for
      if generated pair (p_1, p_2) is not in C **then**
        add generated pair (p_1, p_2) to C as a new concept
      end if
    end for
  end for
  return C

---

5   Applying Automated Generated Concepts to Games

We tried to use the generated concepts to reconstruct heuristic functions. We send queries to a Prolog engine whether each generated concept matches to subsets of simulated playouts. If the query matched, we saved the matching result and counted up how many times it matched. Then we assert a Prolog like heuristic rule of which an evaluation value is the ratio of number of matches frequency to number of subsets as written in Algorithm 3. In our experience, reconstructed heuristic functions are made of only binary relations because all of the generated concepts in Sect. 4 are binary relations on terms.

For Tic-tac-toe, we made heuristic functions from 10,000 random game playouts with each player as the winner, then we evaluated performance using 10,000 simulations against both a random game player and a 1-depth alpha-beta search player. In the results, improvements were seen compared to the player who has no heuristic function, for example, winning ratio of x player improved 14%, but not to players whose heuristic function is better than the 1-body size heuristic function as seen in Tables 3 and 4. We think this is because they lack 1-body and 3-body Prolog rules as we mentioned above.

We also made heuristic functions for Connect Four in the same way. We made two different heuristic functions, one is made from only 10 simulations and the other is made from 100 simulations. Even though only a few simulations, for white player, the generated heuristic functions have good performance. Only 10 simulations are enough to compete with 1-body heuristic functions. 100 simulations are enough to be competitive with 2-body heuristic functions as seen in Tables 3 and 4. This is proof that concepts learned from experience of small games can play bigger games.

We successfully generated new concepts for games from experience of Tic-tac-toe. However, for red player, the result is not good. The difference is that white is the first player and red is the second player. From random game simulation results, it is suggested that the second player has a disadvantage compared to the first player. The difference of performance is possibly due to this property.

Algorithm 3 makeStructuredHeuristics(*concepts*,*playouts*)

---

for all concept c in *concepts* **do**
   $M \Leftarrow$ Hash Map
   for all playout p in *playouts* **do**
      $S \Leftarrow$ getSubset(p)
      for all subset s in S **do**
         if prolog query of c matches to s **then**
            $r \Leftarrow$ matching result of s
            if M contains r **then**
               increment counter for r
            else
               create a hash for r and set the counter as 1
            end if
         end if
         increment the number of subsets *size*
      end for
   end for
   for all m in M **do**
      $v \Leftarrow$ the counter for m / *size*
      add a heuristic, "evaluation(v):-m." into H
   end for
end for
return H

Table 3. Evaluation of heuristic functions made of new concepts for Tic-tac-toe and Connect Four against a random player.

game	player	simulation size	win(%)/lose(%)/draw(%)
Tic-tac-toe	x	10000	94.60/3.77/1.63
	o	10000	56.91/38.05/5.04
Connect Four	white	10	90.6/9.4/0
	white	100	92.3/7.7/0
	red	10	61.8/38.2/0
	red	100	69.4/30.6/0

Table 4. Evaluation of heuristic functions made of new concepts for Tic-tac-toe and Connect Four against a 1-depth alpha-beta search player.

game	player	simulation size	win(%)/lose(%)/draw(%)
Tic-tac-toe	x	10000	89.64/10.36/0
	o	10000	39.16/56.87/3.97
Connect Four	white	10	74.5/25.5/0
	white	100	78.3/21.7/0
	red	10	29.5/70.5/0
	red	100	44.3/55.7/0

6 Automated Generation of Ternary Concepts from Binary Concepts

Generated concepts in Algorithm 2 are relationships between a cell and another cell, i.e., binary relationships. We tried to make ternary relationships as a conjunction of binary relationships. If two binary concepts are satisfied at the same time and a cell is shared in both concepts, the situation is a ternary relationship. Therefore, ternary relationships are made by unification of pairs of terms in each binary concept as written in Algorithm 4.

We generated ternary concepts from the binary concepts generated in Sect. 4. Typical generated concepts are as follows.

$$concept67(X_1, X_2, X_3) : -cell(X_1, X_2, X_3), cell(X_1, X_2 + 1, X_3),$$
$$cell(X_1, X_2 + 2, X_3). \quad (7)$$
$$concept155(X_1, X_2, X_3) : -cell(X_1, X_2, X_3), cell(X_1 + 1, X_2 + 1, X_3),$$
$$cell(X_1 - 1, X_2 - 1, X_3). \quad (8)$$

Equation 7 and 8 represent an idea of line in Tic-tac-toe. Important ternary concepts are successfully generated by this algorithm. The same algorithm has a possibility to make more complex concepts.

We also made heuristic functions made of ternary concepts for Connect Four by Algorithm 3. To reduce generation time, we input 10 simulations and ternary concepts generated as above to Algorithm 3 and made heuristic functions. Then,

---

Algorithm 4 makeTernaryConcepts(*concepts*)

$P \Leftarrow$ makePairsOfConcept(*concepts*)
for all pair (c_1, c_2) in P **do**
  for all term t_1 in body of c_1 **do**
    for all term t_2 in body of c_2 **do**
      if t_1 is able to unificate to t_2 **then**
        $t_3 \Leftarrow$ unification result of t_1 to t_2
        $b_1 \Leftarrow$ make new body as like t_3 appearing in c_1 by unification
        $b_2 \Leftarrow$ make new body as like t_3 appearing in c_2 by unification
        if b_1 is not equals to b_2 **then**
          $R \Leftarrow$ make new concept by conjunction of b_1 and b_2
        end if
      end if
    end for
  end for
end for
$R \Leftarrow$ remove overlap from R
return R

Table 5. Evaluation of heuristic functions made of ternary concepts for Connect Four against a random player.

game	player	simulation size	win(%)/lose(%)/draw(%)
Connect Four	white	10	72.7/27.3/0
	red	10	71.7/28.3/0

Table 6. Evaluation of heuristic functions made of ternary concepts for Connect Four against a 1-depth alpha-beta search player.

game	player	simulation size	win(%)/lose(%)/draw(%)
Connect Four	white	10	39.7/60.3/0
	red	10	37.8/62.2/0

we evaluated it using 1,000 simulations against a random game player or a 1-depth alpha-beta search player. Results are not good as seen in Table 5 and 6. We think this is due to noises from less important concepts. In Algorithm 3, all input concepts are concerned, therefore, not only important concepts like Eq. 7 or 8 but also less important concepts affect evaluation values. This result suggests a limitation of Algorithm 3 and a need for better algorithm.

7   Discussion

In this study, we successfully extracted the essential concepts included in the game automatically. The proposed algorithm is applicable to general games. The algorithm learns new concepts without any supervised signals but from experience in a certain environment. The generated concepts are fundamental features of the environment, and can be used to play some games with different rules.

A typical concept learned in this study is as follows.

$$concept(X_0, X_1, X_2) : -cell(X_0, X_1, X_2), cell(X_0, X_1 + 1, X_2). \qquad (9)$$

This concept is applicable to all games in which players put a mark or piece on a two-dimensional board. Even more, through appropriate filters, it is possible to apply the concept to computer vision to understand semantics of a picture. If one makes a filter which converts a picture to Prolog like facts, this concept is applicable for recognizing semantics of series of squares with contents. In other words, concepts generated in this study are available to understand semantics of our living world, not only of artificial game worlds.

It is necessary for a human being to input supervised signals when an artificial intelligence learns concepts about our living world. For example, when we do Natural Language Processing to generate ontology, we need to input well written texts which are written by human beings [10]. It is impossible to learn ontology from automatically generated strings. However, in this study, we successfully generated concepts about our world without any supervised signals by human beings. This property is due to the special advantage of games, i.e., environments having concrete rules. In other words, human beings do not have to judge a meaning of record of random games because a simulator is able to judge it, i.e., who is the winner according to its game rules. This tremendously desirable advantage is available only in games, not in other fields. In our study, it is proven that we are able to generate essential concepts about our living world from games according to the advantage.

8   Conclusions

In our study, we automatically generated concepts which were applicable to understand the world of the games for General Game Playing. Obtained concepts were general and useful to understand several games. General Game Playing is a desirable research area for automatically learning concepts of our living world. To apply obtained concepts to more games and to generate more complex concepts are the problems which remain to be solved.

Acknowledgments. The authors would like to express their appreciation to Mr. Abdallah Saffidine for his contribution to the stimulating discussions, Prof. Erick Alphonse for his comments on Inductive Logic Programming, Prof. Hiroyuki Iida and Japan Advanced Institute of Science and Technology for funding and Dr. Kristian Spoerer for proof reading.

References

1. Björnsson, Y., Finnsson, H.: CADIAPLAYER: a simulation-based general game player. IEEE Trans. Comput. Intell. AI Games **1**, 4–15 (2009)

2. Clune, J.: Heuristic evaluation functions for general game playing. In: Proceedings of the National Conference on Artificial Intelligence, pp. 1134–1139 (2007)
3. Finnsson, H., Björnsson, Y.: Simulation-based approach to general game playing. In: Proceedings of the Twenty-Third AAAI Conference on Artificial Intelligence, pp. 259–264 (2008)
4. Inoue, K., Furukawa, K., Kobayashi.: Abducing rules with predicate invention. In: The 19th International Conference on Inductive Logic Programming (2009)
5. Kaneko, T., Yamaguchi, K., Kawai, S.: Automatic feature construction and optimization for general game player. In: Proceedings of Game Programming Workshop 2001, pp. 25–32 (2001)
6. Kirci, M., Sturtevant, N., Schaeffer, J.: A GGP feature learning algorithm. KI - Künstliche Intell. **25**, 35–42 (2011)
7. Love, N., Hinrichs, T., Haley, D., Schkufza, E., Genesereth, M.: General game playing: game description language specification. http://games.stanford.edu/readings/gdl_spec.pdf (2008)
8. Méhat, J., Cazenave, T.: A parallel general game player. KI-Künstliche Intell. **25**, 43–47 (2011)
9. Michulke, D., Thielscher, M.: Neural networks for state evaluation in general game playing. In: Buntine, W., Grobelnik, M., Mladenić, D., Shawe-Taylor, J. (eds.) ECML PKDD 2009, Part II. LNCS(LNAI), vol. 5782, pp. 95–110. Springer, Heidelberg (2009)
10. Mohamed, T.P., Hruschka, E.R.J., Mitchell, T.M.: Discovering relations between noun categories. In: Proceedings of the Conference on Empirical Methods in Natural Language Processing, pp. 1447–1455 (2011)
11. Schiffel, S.: http://www.general-game-playing.de/index.html (2008)
12. Skowronski, P., Björnsson, Y., Winands, H.M.M.: Automated discovery of search-control features. In: Proceedings of the Twelfth International Advances in Computer Games Conference, pp. 182–194 (2009)

WALTZ: A Strong Tzaar-Playing Program

Tomáš Valla[1] and Pavel Veselý[2]([⊠])

[1] Faculty of Information Technology,
Czech Technical University in Prague, Praha 6, Czech Republic
tomas.valla@fit.cvut.cz
[2] Faculty of Mathematics and Physics,
Charles University in Prague, Praha 1, Czech Republic
vesely@iuuk.mff.cuni.cz

Abstract. Tzaar is an abstract strategy two-player game, which has recently gained popularity in the gaming community and has won several awards. There are some properties, most notably the high branching factor, that make Tzaar hard for computers. We developed WALTZ, a strong Tzaar-playing program, using enhanced variants of Alpha-beta and Proof-number Search based algorithms. After many tests with computer opponents and a year of deployment on a popular board-gaming portal, we conclude that WALTZ can defeat all available computer programs and even strong human players. In this paper we describe WALTZ, its performance and an enhancement of Proof-number Search developed for WALTZ that can be also used in other domains than Tzaar.

1 Introduction

Tzaar is a relatively new game, which was invented by Kris Burm and published in 2007. Despite being so young, Tzaar has won quite a lot of awards, most notably the Games Magazine's award "Game of the Year 2009" [19], "Spiel des Jahres" Recommendation in 2008 [21], and earned nominations to several other awards. Tzaar is also highly rated by the gaming community, for example on the popular server BoardGameGeek.com it has the second highest rating among abstract games. It is a part of the Project GIPF, a set of six abstract strategy two-player games. The first game of the project, also called GIPF, was played on Computer Olympiad [20] in 2001.

There are several properties that make Tzaar a hard game to play for computers. Most notably it is the high branching factor (see Sect. 1.3). Even in the endgame there is usually more than one solution to a threat, thus algorithms based on threats like Dependency-based Search [1] or Lambda Search [10] are not effective. We cannot also easily decompose the game into independent parts (unlike Amazons), thus standard techniques from combinatorial game theory are not applicable. Therefore, writing a strong Tzaar playing program is a challenge. We address this challenge by developing WALTZ,[1] a strong program able

---

Tomáš Valla—This work was supported by the Centre of Excellence—Inst. for Theor. Comp. Sci. (project P202/12/G061 of GA ČR).
[1] The name stands for the recursive acronym *Waltz ALgorithmic TZaar*.

T. Cazenave et al. (Eds.): CGW 2013, CCIS 408, pp. 81–96, 2014.
DOI: 10.1007/978-3-319-05428-5_7, © Springer International Publishing Switzerland 2014

to defeat all other Tzaar programs that we are aware of, and also—which is more important—match up with and defeat even strong human players.

We have installed several playable "robots" on the popular board-gaming portal Boitejeaux.net [18], where some very strong players are playing. The details about WALTZ performance against both computer and human opponents can be found in Sect. 4.

The algorithms employed in WALTZ are based on Alpha-beta pruning and Proof-number Search (PNS), together with many enhancements, see Sect. 2 for more details. We chose and tuned these algorithms and their enhancements after numerous statistical experiments and play-outs with other Tzaar playing programs, humans, and different versions of WALTZ.

We also developed an enhancement of PNS for WALTZ called Heuristic Weak PNS. See Sect. 2.2 for its description.

This paper was preceded by the thesis of Veselý [13], which, although slightly outdated, contains a lot of details that are omitted here. WALTZ, the thesis, and other information can be downloaded from our website [11].

1.1 Tzaar Rules

Tzaar is a modern abstract strategy two-player game with full information, bearing a distant similarity to Checkers in some sense.

The board for Tzaar is hexagonal and consists of 30 lines that makes 60 intersections. There is a missing intersection in the center of the board. In the starting position there are 30 white and 30 black pieces, one at each intersection. Each color has pieces of three types: 6 are *Tzaars,* 9 are *Tzarras* and 15 are *Totts.* See Fig. 1 for illustration.

The initial placement could be random or players can use a fixed starting position which is defined in the official rules [2].

Pieces can form *stacks,* that means, towers of pieces of the same color. In the beginning, all stacks on the board have height one. A stack is one entity, thus it cannot be divided into two stacks. The type of a stack is the type of its top piece.

White player and black player take turns, white has the first turn. Each player's turn consists of two moves. There is an exception in the very first turn of white player, as his turn consists only of the first move.

The first move of each turn must be a *capture.* The player on turn moves one of his stacks along a line to an intersection with an opponent's stack. A stack cannot jump over other stacks or over the center of the board. Only a jump over an arbitrary number of empty intersections is allowed. No stack may end the jump on an empty intersection. A captured stack must have height at most the height of the capturing stack. Captured pieces leave the board.

The second move of a turn can be another capture move, or a stacking move, or a pass move. *Passing* means that the player on turn does not move with any stack. During the *stacking move* the player jumps with his stack on some other stack of his color. The height of the resulting stack is the sum of both stacks heights. The type of the resulting stack is determined by the piece on the top.

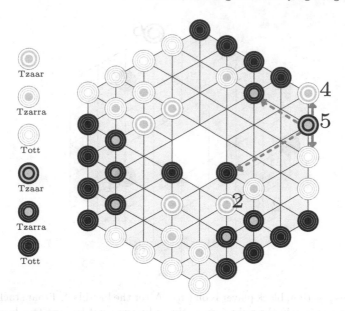

Fig. 1. The Tzaar board with a sample position and piece types on the left. The possible moves of the black Tzaar stack in the second move of a turn are marked by arrows, the dashed arrows represent stacking moves and the numbers denote the stack heights greater than one.

A player loses when the last stack of one of the three types is captured, or if he cannot capture in the first move of his turn. A draw is not possible.

1.2   Strategies

In this section we discuss some common heuristic strategies how to play Tzaar. These observations are based on authors' experiences from numerous play-outs with both human and computer opponents. We use these strategies to construct the evaluation function of WALTZ, see Sect. 2.1. However, as these strategies are based on heuristic arguments, there are of course positions where they do not yield good results.

The first move is always a capture move, but it often depends which type of piece is captured. A good move usually consists of capturing piece type t such that the opponent does not have a high stack of type t, and as a secondary condition such type t that there are not many stacks of type t. In a typical game the player starts by creating a stack of Tzaar, it is thus convenient to capture Tzarras.

In the second move of a turn a player has three possibilities:

– *Capturing* again (so called *double-capture move*). This is appropriate if the opponent is running out of pieces of a certain type (he should not have a high stack of that type), or if a high stack can be captured. Height of the double captured stack should be greater than two, because by capturing stacks of size

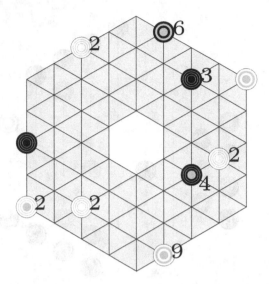

Fig. 2. In this position, black player is on turn. After the last black Tzaar stack captures the white Tzaar piece in the right corner, the only move not leading to a loss for black is the pass move.

two, a player may lose capturing possibilities. Moreover, double capturing two pieces with height one usually leads to a loss because of no capturing possibilities.

– *Stacking* is often the most reasonable move, because it makes one of the stacks more powerful and more safe against opponent's stacks. The other reason is that the opponent loses capturing possibilities, thus it is more likely that he will run out of captures and lose in the endgame.

– *Passing* occurs rarely during the game. It is worth playing only in the endgame when stacking and capturing are not possible or would result in a loss. See Fig. 2 for an example of such position.

There are generally two stacking strategies:

1. Creating one high stack which is powerful and can capture all opponent's stacks, or which forces the opponent to raise his highest stack.
2. Creating more lower stacks, usually of height two, although it is safer when some of them have height at least three.

It is not known to us which strategy is better. Using the first strategy the player can quite easily threaten or even capture small opponent's stacks, but using the second strategy it is sometimes impossible for the opponent to create a new stack (it would be captured immediately) and the opponent can lose because of it. The second strategy is more reasonable during the endgame, since it decreases the opponent's capturing possibilities. Also, having a stack much higher than all other opponent's stacks is worse than having more lower stacks.

These strategy observations were mostly about material; now we give some positional strategy tips:

– Keeping high stacks inside the board, not on the border. Stacks inside are able to move to any direction and thus they threaten large part of the board. Moreover, during the middle game a stack placed inside the board can nearly always escape from a threat. The worst positions are the six corners of the board.
– Limiting moving possibilities of an opponent's high stack, i.e., moving pieces away from lines containing an opponent's high stack.
– Isolating a small stack (preferably of size one) such that there are no other pieces on the same lines as the isolated stack. The reason is that the player cannot run out of the type of an isolated piece, thus the type is safe.
– Isolating own high stack is not good, because the stack cannot be used for capturing opponent's stacks.
– Limiting opponent's capturing possibilities and also preparing own capturing possibilities during the endgame.

The black player has a small advantage, because he is stacking first. Hence he can often threaten white player by attacking white stacks and white player should create his first stack as far from black player's stack as possible.

1.3   Game Properties

We estimate the maximum height of a stack. Observe that before a stacking move that created a stack of height h, the opponent must have captured at least $h - 1$ pieces. There should be two pieces of another types present and there are 30 pieces of each color, the maximum number of captures is 13 as at least two other pieces must be present, so the maximum stack height is 14.

The *state space complexity* is the number of game positions reachable from any starting position. There are $\binom{60}{v}$ different choices of fields for stacks, where v is the number of free fields. Let k be the sum of heights of all white stacks on the board, i.e. the number of white pieces, and analogously ℓ for the black color. Both numbers are bounded from above by the number of necessary captures before exactly v free fields appeared on the board. Thus $k, \ell \le 30 - \lfloor \frac{1}{4}v \rfloor$ (at least one fourth of moves must capture a white stack).

Let there be s white stacks, so the number of black stacks is $60 - v - s$. We know that $s \le \min(k, 58 - v)$, since there are k white pieces and there must be two black stacks on $60 - v$ occupied fields on the board. The number of different stack heights for s stacks with k white pieces is $\binom{k-1}{s-1}$; the number of different choices of fields for white stacks is $\binom{60-v}{s}$ and 3^s is the number of different types of white stacks. Similar formulas hold for black player. This gives us the upper bound on the number of possible states:

$$\sum_{v=1}^{55} \binom{60}{v} \sum_{k=2}^{30-\lfloor \frac{1}{4}v \rfloor} \sum_{s=2}^{\min(k,58-v)} \binom{60-v}{s}\binom{k-1}{s-1}3^s \cdot \sum_{\ell=60-v-s}^{30-\lfloor \frac{1}{4}v \rfloor} \binom{\ell-1}{59-v-s}3^{60-s-v}$$

$$\doteq 9.17 \cdot 10^{57}$$

Let us now take symmetries into account. The position can have 6 equivalent rotations. The position may also have 6 isomorphic mirrors by 6 axes (between opposite corners of the board and between centers of opposite sides). Mirroring twice by any two axes results in a rotated position, thus there are 12 isomorphic positions. We use Burnside's Lemma (the orbit-counting theorem) to count the number of distinct positions.

For each symmetry we estimate the number of fixed points, i.e., positions that are the same after applying a symmetry. The identity has clearly $9.17 \cdot 10^{57}$ fixed points. Rotation symmetries (except identity) have at most $(14 \cdot 6 + 1)^{10} \doteq 1.97 \cdot 10^{19}$ fixed points, since the maximal height is 14, Tzaar has six types of pieces and the six triangles with 10 fields that lie between the side of the board and the side of the empty part in the middle must be the same. Mirroring by axes has at most $4.83 \cdot 10^{28}$ fixed points which we obtain using similar formula as for the state space complexity. From Burnside's Lemma we get the upper bound on the number of distinct positions reachable from any starting position:

$$(9.17 \cdot 10^{57} + 5 \cdot 1.97 \cdot 10^{19} + 6 \cdot 4.83 \cdot 10^{28})/12 = 7.64 \cdot 10^{56}$$

This is an upper bound on the number of positions that can be reached from all starting positions altogether, but some positions can be obtained from more than one initial position.

The number of different starting positions is $60!/(15! \cdot 9! \cdot 6!)^2 \doteq 7.13 \cdot 10^{40}$. Using Burnside's Lemma to deal with symmetries we get $5.94 \cdot 10^{39}$ different starting positions. The number of fixed points is zero for rotation symmetries, since the number of black Totts is not divisible by six. For mirroring symmetries the number of fixed points is at most $30!/(8! \cdot 5! \cdot 3!)^2 \doteq 3.15 \cdot 10^{17}$.

Let us now estimate the number of endgame positions. We count the number of positions with six stacks of different types or colors—if there are two pieces of the same color and type, the position is won by one of the players. We observe that the number of positions with more than six stacks is higher. The number of positions with exactly six stacks is the number of different choices of six fields on the board multiplied by the number of permutations of six stacks and the number of different stack sizes for each piece type and for each player. The maximum sum of stack sizes for a player is 16, because there should be a capture before each stacking. Therefore, the number of endgame positions is

$$\binom{60}{6} \cdot 6! \cdot \left(\sum_{i=3}^{16} \binom{i-1}{2} \right)^2 \doteq 1.13 \cdot 10^{16},$$

where i denotes the sum of stack heights for one player.

After taking symmetries into account, we get $9.42 \cdot 10^{14}$ different positions with six different stacks. Note that the number of fixed points is zero for rotations symmetries and for mirroring by axes between opposite sides. For mirroring between opposite corners it is at most

$$6! \cdot \left(\sum_{i=3}^{16} \binom{i-1}{2} \right)^2 \doteq 2.26 \cdot 10^8$$

Table 1. Minimum, maximum and average branching factor according to the number of stacks on the board. The table contains also the number of positions from which the values were obtained. We sampled positions from real games at BAJ [18] and these positions can be downloaded from [11].

Stacks	59	55	49	43	37	31	25	19	13	9	7	6
positions	470	464	456	460	446	427	399	338	170	61	15	7
Minimum	4961	3962	2732	1732	906	403	139	35	1	1	1	1
Maximum	9933	7651	6007	4235	2986	2078	1073	476	114	21	4	2
Average	7497	5965	4463	2971	1978	1117	562	203	37	7	1	1

For a lower bound on the state space complexity we can use the number of distinct starting positions which is $5.94 \cdot 10^{39}$. We thus believe that the real state space complexity lies roughly between 10^{45} and 10^{55}.

The *branching factor* depends on the starting position. The fixed starting position has the maximum branching factor around 5 500, but there are starting positions with the branching factor up to 10 000. We count positions reachable by two possible ways only once, otherwise the branching factor can be 14 000. During the game, the branching factor is decreasing as the pieces are captured or stacked. Table 1 provides a summary of the minimum, maximum and average branching factor according to the number of stacks on the board, computed statistically from real play-outs.

The *game tree complexity* is usually estimated by multiplying the average branching factor for each turn. For Tzaar we get approximately 10^{79}.

We conclude that Tzaar has much larger state space complexity than GIPF that has roughly 10^{25} different positions [14] and probably slightly larger than Chess that has 10^{46} positions [3]. The game is also harder for computers because of huge number of possible starting positions and more importantly the branching factor which is more than 1000 for most of the game. In contrast, GIPF or Chess have average branching factor from 30 to 40. On the other hand, Tzaar games are quite short, typically up to 28 turns of a player, thus the game tree of Chess or GIPF is larger (about 10^{123} for Chess and 10^{132} for GIPF [14]).

2   Algorithms for Tzaar

We now discuss algorithms we have implemented in WALTZ. We also describe domain dependent heuristics. Since the game tree properties differ in the middle game and in the endgame, we discuss these parts of the game separately.

Due to the high number of possible starting positions the Opening database technique is not applicable. Similarly, one cannot use the endgame database as even the number of positions with only six different stacks is $9.42 \cdot 10^{14}$ as we counted in Sect. 1.3. We thus believe that data-base methods are not applicable in Tzaar.

We cannot also easily decompose the game into independent parts, since stacks can jump from one part of the board to another by few moves. Hence standard techniques from combinatorial game theory are not applicable.

Opening has the highest branching factor, but otherwise it is not very different from the middle game. Before the endgame, the attacking player usually cannot capture defender's high stack or even win in a few moves by a threat sequence. Defender can escape with his stack from most threats easily and there are often more different ways to do it. We thus conclude that algorithms based on threats would be ineffective during the opening and middle game, therefore Proof-number Search (PNS) is used only during the endgame.

The most frequently used algorithm in WALTZ is Minimax with the Alpha-beta pruning and several enhancements, namely:

- Transposition Table (TT): Used for storing moves from the previous shallower search (the Principal Variation Move, PV) and also because some positions can be reached by a few different move sequences.
- Iterative Deepening (ID): Implemented because of time estimation (how deep may the engine search), and because of PV.
- domain specific Move Ordering (MO): Done by heuristically assigning values to moves and sorting moves according to these values. In most cases, stacking is preferred to capturing.
- History Heuristic (HH): Only for the first move of a turn.
- NegaScout (NS): To quickly find cutoff nodes.
- Randomized Alpha-beta: for the first two moves, WALTZ chooses uniformly randomly among moves with a value at least $bestValue - margin$ for a given constant $margin$. These moves are found using a slightly modified Alpha-beta search. See [13] for more details.
- Playing in lost positions: when WALTZ finds out that it is in a lost position, it uses the best move in the last iteration of the Iterative Deepening where Alpha-beta has not found out that the position is lost. Thus WALTZ plays a move that leads to a loss after the maximal possible number of moves.

In the endgame the branching factor is not so high and threat sequences occur more frequently. There are also fewer solutions to threats, thus threats limit the branching factor and Proof-number Search (PNS) can sometimes be more effective than Alpha-beta search. However, PNS as proposed by Allis [1] consumes a considerable amount of memory. Therefore, we use the Depth-first Proof-number Search (DFPN) [6] with the following enhancements:

- Move Ordering: The same as in Alpha-beta.
- Evaluation Function Based PNS (EFB PNS) [15]: Heuristic initialization of leaves using the evaluation function.
- $1 + \varepsilon$ Trick [7]: To avoid frequent jumping of the search across the tree.
- Weak PNS (WPNS) [4] and Dynamic Widening (DW) [17]: To suppress overestimation of proof and disproof numbers.
- Heuristic Weak PNS (HW PNS): A new enhancement, see Sect. 2.2.

- Time estimation: How many nodes can DFPN visit within a given time—at first a certain number of nodes is visited and then the number of nodes to visit is estimated.

We note that there are some other algorithms for solving endgame positions. For the Lambda Search [10] we were not able to determine quickly the order of a threat. Since there is usually more than one way to evade a threat, we may conclude that the Dependency-based Search [1] is not suitable for Tzaar.

See Sect. 3 for an evaluation of how each enhancement improves the search. The detailed description of the algorithms and their enhancements can be found e.g. in [13].

2.1   Evaluation Function

The evaluation of a position in Tzaar is used both by the Alpha-beta search and DFPN. We created the evaluation function according to strategy observations given in Sect. 1.2. We tuned up its constants by playing with WALTZ and by numerous play-outs between different versions of the evaluation function.

In positions with a positive value, white player has an advantage (∞ is a win), and vice versa for black player. We basically use this formula:

$$\text{eval}(position) = \text{material}(position, \text{White}) + \text{positional}(position, \text{White})$$
$$- \text{material}(position, \text{Black}) - \text{positional}(position, \text{Black})$$

The material value for a player is the sum of values of player's stacks:

$$\text{material}(position, player) = \sum_{\substack{s \text{ is a stack} \\ \text{of } player}} \text{heightValue}(s) \cdot \text{countValue}(s)$$

The function heightValue grows rapidly up to 150 for heights less than 4, then stays nearly the same and decreases for stacks higher than 8. The reason is that instead of building very high stacks a player can build more lower stacks, which is usually better. The function countValue is inversely proportional to the count of stacks with the same piece type as the stack s. It is 100 for the count 1, then it decreases rapidly and it is less than 20 for counts higher than 5.

The material value is more important in the first half of the game. The material value together with some positional information is counted incrementally (when a move is executed or reverted), other positional features are counted statically for each leaf node that is not won by a player.

For the positional value the Zone of Control (ZOC) is maintained. It determines how many stacks of a certain type can be captured in one move, no matter who is on turn. It is used also for determining whether a player on turn has lost because of no possible captures.

The positional value for a player is roughly the sum of these bonuses:

- 20 000 000 for an immediate threat: The player is on turn and he can capture all stacks of an opponent's piece type (the player can win).

- 1 000 for a threat, when the player is not on turn.
- 1 000–200 000 if the opponent has few possible captures.
- Value of ZOC: $\sum_{\substack{\text{opponent's} \\ \text{piece type } t}}$ stacksInZOC$(t) \cdot (1 - \text{count}(t)/\text{initialCount}(t))$
- 25 000 for each player's piece type that is "secure"—the player has a stack higher than all stacks of his opponent—and 100 000 if all types are secure.
- 50 000 for stacks with height at least 2 of all types.
- 50 000 if an opponent's valuable stack can be captured.
- 1 000–100 000 for an opponent's high stack that cannot move.
- 10–25 for high stacks not on the margin of the board and −30 for a stack in the corner.

2.2   Heuristic Weak PNS

As positions often occur more than once in a game, the state space is described by a directed acyclic graph instead of a tree. Then DFPN suffers from the *double-counting problem*, when the proof number of a position contains the proof number of another position more than once.

This problem can be addressed by modifying the summation of disproof numbers in OR nodes and proof numbers in AND nodes. Weak PNS [4] proposes taking the maximum disproof number and adding the number of children minus one. Another solution to this problem is described by Kishimoto [5].

We propose a new enhancement based on Weak PNS and the evaluation function. We modify counting disproof numbers in OR nodes (and analogously in AND nodes) in a way similar to Evaluation Function Based PNS. The idea of using the evaluation function is also briefly mentioned by Kishimoto [5].

We define the step function similarly to Evaluation Function Based PNS:

$$\text{step}(value) = \begin{cases} 2 & \text{if } value \geq t, \\ 1 & \text{if } -t < value < t, \\ 0 & \text{if } value \leq -t, \end{cases}$$

where *value* is the value of the current position and the threshold t indicates the player's high advantage. The best value for t is at least 10^6 (see Sect. 3) while a win has value $2 \cdot 10^9$.

We count the disproof number (DN) as $maxDN + h(m-1)\,\text{step}(value)$, where $maxDN$ is the maximum disproof number among children, m is the number of moves and $h > 0$ is a constant.

Now we discuss reasons for this modification of Weak PNS. When the player on turn has a big advantage and $value \geq t$, DN is ∞ with a high probability. We can thus set DN to $maxDN + 2h(m - 1)$. In the case of a balanced position, we count DN similarly to Weak PNS. Because of this, the parameter h should be close to 1. When the player on turn is in a bad position, we likely do not need to search many positions to disprove the node, so DN is set to $maxDN$.

3 Experiments with WALTZ

This section shows the results of search runtime optimization. For parameter tuning and measuring the runtime we use two sets of Tzaar positions. The first set, we call it *MidSet*, consists of 200 middle game positions with exactly 41 stacks on the board. It is intended for testing Alpha-beta.

For experimenting with DFPN we have a set of 713 endgame positions with less than 27 stacks on the board, we call it *EndSet*. This set contains both easy positions (WALTZ solves them quickly) and hard positions (neither DFPN, nor Alpha-beta are able to find a solution within a minute). Both *MidSet* and *EndSet* are available at [11]. We took these positions from WALTZ's games with strong and intermediate players on BAJ.

We performed the tests on a Dual-Core AMD Opteron 2216 server with 64 GiB of memory, but we used only one of its cores.

For Alpha-beta we measured the efficiency of the Alpha-beta enhancements in the domain of Tzaar by searching each *MidSet* position to the depth of 3 turns. We observed that it is best to use all Alpha-beta enhancements listed in Sect. 2. Since this behavior occurs also in other games, this approach does not contribute with some new insight, so we omit the exact results. They can be found in [13].

Table 2 shows the importance of enhancements for DFPN. Note that there is nearly no difference between DW, WPNS and HW PNS, and that one single enhancement is still not enough. Surprisingly, sorting moves heuristically using the same algorithm as in Alpha-beta is useful. We ran the tests on *EndSet* positions with the time limit of 60 s.

We find it strange that Heuristic Weak PNS does not solve more positions than Weak PNS, but we think that Heuristic Weak PNS can improve solvers in other games.

We experimented also with different sizes of TT and constants used in DFPN enhancements, namely Heuristic Weak PNS, $1 + \varepsilon$ Trick, EFB PNS and DW. For each constant we tried different values, run the experiments and counted the number of solved positions from *EndSet*. The results are omitted due to space limitations and can be found in [13].

Table 2. Results of the DFPN search with different enhancements listed in Sect. 2.

Enhancements	Solved (out of 713)
HW, $1 + \varepsilon$ Trick and EFB	484
WPNS, $1 + \varepsilon$ Trick and EFB	484
DW, $1 + \varepsilon$ Trick and EFB	480
HW, $1 + \varepsilon$ Trick and EFB without sorting moves	465
Only $1 + \varepsilon$ Trick	343
Without enhancements	336
Only Heuristic Weak (HW)	289
Only Evaluation Function Based (EFB)	289

Heuristic Weak PNS has two parameters: the threshold t for the step function and the multiplier h. From the experiments we observed that the best values are $h = 1$ and $t \geq 10^6$—the value of a position in which a player has a significant advantage.

3.1 DFPN versus Alpha-beta in Endgames

DFPN was designed to find long winning strategies where the player can force his opponent to have only a limited number of possible moves. We tried DFPN on Tzaar endgames, although Tzaar has relatively high branching factor even in endgames. On the other hand, the player can sometimes force his opponent to have a small number of moves.

To decide whether to use Alpha-beta or DFPN in endgames we ran statistical experiments. Using the best possible setting of constants in DFPN, it solved 495 out of 713 positions. Then we tried Alpha-beta (with all enhancements) and it solved 506 positions. There are 20 positions which DFPN solved and Alpha-beta did not, so DFPN is reasonable to use in WALTZ.

Hence WALTZ try to use DFPN first in the endgame when the number of stacks is at most 23. If it does not succeed because of the time limit or because DFPN found disproof, we run the Alpha-beta search.

4   Results Against Computer and Human Opponents

We tested WALTZ against other existing programs for playing Tzaar that are available: HsTZAAR [12] and programs of students from University of Alaska [22].[2] See Table 3 for the results.

During the tests, WALTZ had a time limit of 30 s. Each game started with a random starting position. We performed tests with HsTZAAR on Intel Xeon ES-1620 server with 64 GiB of memory and tests with the other programs on a AMD Turion II P560 Dual-Core notebook with 4 GiB of memory.

To test WALTZ against people we chose the game server Boiteajeux.net (BAJ) [18], since a lot of people play Tzaar there.[3] For each game, an ELO rating is counted.[4]

We created four different versions of WALTZ which are described in Table 4. We performed matches between these versions to compare their strength. See Table 5 for the results.

Now we describe how successful WALTZ was against human opponents on BAJ. We focus only on the expert and unbeatable versions since the other versions are intended to play weaker.

---

[2] There are also some more programs available, but due to their design it is not possible to run automatic play-outs between them and WALTZ.

[3] 299 players have played Tzaar in the last six month till May 10, 2013 and 24 842 Tzaar games were finished on BAJ from October 31, 2008 to May 10, 2013.

[4] For a win a player obtains some ELO points according to his and opponent's ELO and his opponent loses the same number of points. New player receives ELO 1 500.

Table 3. Results of WALTZ against other Tzaar-playing programs. Wins and losses are counted from the WALTZ's point of view.

Program	Wins	Losses	Note
HsTZAAR	479	121	Used with the algorithm `pscout_full_4` on 4 cores
GreensteinTzaarAI	342	53	We could not set a time limit
BiTzaarBot	196	5	The time limit was 40 s
Mockinator++	83	2	The time limit was 40 s
Mockinator	82	1	The time limit was 40 s

Table 4. Versions of WALTZ.

Level	Username on BAJ	Time limit [s]	Used algorithms
Beginner	PauliebotBeginner	30	RandomizedAlpha-beta with a big margin (5000) and a very simple evaluation function to the depth of two turns of a player for the whole game
Intermediate	PauliebotMedium	30	RandomizedAlpha-beta with a small margin (20) and the full evaluation function to the depth of two and half turns for the whole game
Expert	Pauliebot	30	BothAlpha-beta and DFPN with the full evaluation function
"Unbeatable"	PauliebotUnbeatable	300	BothAlpha-beta and DFPN with the full evaluation function

Table 5. Results of matches between versions of WALTZ.

	Beginner	Intermediate	Expert	"Unbeatable"
Beginner		224:1140	218:1090	45:351
Intermediate	1140:224		647:1371	84:208
Expert	1090:218	1371:647		98:149
"Unbeatable"	351:45	208:84	149:98	

We released WALTZ in the expert version on March 20, 2012 under username *Pauliebot*, and it was under development until April 4, 2012. After that we made only minor updates, mostly improving the evaluation function. On April 24, 2012 we released the other versions of WALTZ.

The expert version has played 154 games so far.[5] It won 114 of them and it is the 16th best Tzaar player with ELO 2 068.[6] Most important results of the expert version are in the left part of Table 6. We conclude that the expert version

---

[5] Some of these games were played for testing purposes.

[6] ELOs of players and other data in this section were up to the date March 4, 2013.

Table 6. Some results of the expert (left) and unbeatable (right) versions. Wins and losses are counted from the WALTZ's point of view. Note that Paulie is a nickname of one of the authors, not of one of the WALTZ's version.

Player	Rank	ELO	Wins	Losses
SlowBrain	1st	2 432	1	3
Gambit	2nd	2 229	2	4
Paulie	3rd	2 220	8	3
evrardmoloic	17th	2 062	1	1
mat76	77th	1 690	16	1
Gregg	78th	1 684	14	5
PhilDakota	79th	1 684	14	3

Player	Rank	ELO	Wins	Losses
SlowBrain	1st	2 432	9	16
Paulie	3rd	2 220	1	3
mnmr	6th	2 184	0	1
Zeichner	9th	2 143	1	0
Talisac	13th	2 100	3	0
azazhel	28th	1 931	8	2

played on the level of best players on BAJ, but sometimes intermediate players were able to defeat it.

The unbeatable WALTZ version has ELO 2087, the 14th highest, and played 74 games from which it won 46 games.[7] The most important results of the unbeatable version are in the right part of Table 6. The 9 wins against SlowBrain are a great success because SlowBrain is far better than other players. From these results we conclude that more time to search helps WALTZ to play better.

The most frequently appearing reason why WALTZ lost games on BAJ was the loss of the last stack of Tzarras. We observed that in two or three last turns of these lost games WALTZ had no chance to create a stack of Tzarras which could not be captured by the opponent—WALTZ was probably not aware of such an opponent's trap soon enough. Another bad thing in WALTZ's behavior during these games was losing quite high stacks (size 3, 4, or even 5) during the middle game.

We thus tried to improve the evaluation function to avoid these problems. The version with the enhanced evaluation function won 136 and lost 102 games against the version with the old evaluation function. On March 4, 2013 we released the version with the enhanced evaluation function.

5 Further Work

There are some other algorithms which we did not implement in WALTZ. Monte Carlo Tree Search is probably the most promising approach, and we consider it to be the next direction where we would like to move WALTZ's development. Another direction lies in parallelizing WALTZ's algorithms, which is a natural step we would like to try. For example the DFPN algorithm can be parallelized by Job-level Proof-number search [16], there are also parallelization approaches proposed by Saito, Winands and van den Herik [9], or Saffidine, Jouandeau and Cazenave [8].

---

[7] Some of these games were against other WALTZ versions—this was done to increase robot's ELO, otherwise strong players would not want to play against an opponent with a low ELO.

It turned out that the enhancement Heuristic Weak PNS was not better than Weak PNS in the domain of Tzaar, but we leave for a future research whether it can be useful in other domains.

References

1. Allis, L.V.: Searching for solutions in games and artificial intelligence. Ph.D. thesis, University of Limburg, Maastricht, The Netherlands (1994)
2. Burm, K.: Tzaar rules. GIPF Project. http://www.gipf.com/tzaar/rules/rules.html
3. Chinchalkar, S.: An upper bound for the number of reachable positions. ICCA J. **19**(3), 181–183 (1996)
4. Ueda, T., Hashimoto, T., Hashimoto, J., Iida, H.: Weak Proof-number search. In: van den Herik, H.J., Xu, X., Ma, Z., Winands, M.H.M. (eds.) CG 2008. LNCS, vol. 5131, pp. 157–168. Springer, Heidelberg (2008)
5. Kishimoto, A.: Dealing with infinite loops, underestimation, and overestimation of depth-first proof-number search. In: Fox, M., Poole, D. (eds.) Proceedings of the Twenty-Fourth AAAI Conference on Artificial Intelligence, AAAI 2010, Atlanta, Georgia, USA. AAAI Press (2010)
6. Nagai, A.: Df-pn algorithm for searching AND/OR trees and its applications. Ph.D. thesis, The University of Tokyo, Japan (2002)
7. Pawlewicz, J., Lew, Ł.: Improving depth-first PN-search: 1 + ε trick. In: van den Herik, H.J., Ciancarini, P., Donkers, H.H.L.M.J. (eds.) CG 2006. LNCS, vol. 4630, pp. 160–171. Springer, Heidelberg (2007)
8. Saffidine, A., Jouandeau, N., Cazenave, T.: Solving BREAKTHROUGH with race patterns and job-level proof number search. In: van den Herik, H.J., Plaat, A. (eds.) ACG 2011. LNCS, vol. 7168, pp. 196–207. Springer, Heidelberg (2012)
9. Saito, J.-T., Winands, M.H.M., van den Herik, H.J.: Randomized parallel proof-number search. In: van den Herik, H.J., Spronck, P. (eds.) ACG 2009. LNCS, vol. 6048, pp. 75–87. Springer, Heidelberg (2010)
10. Thomsen, T.: Lambda-search in game trees - with application to go. ICGA J. **23**(4), 203–217 (2001). (Springer)
11. Valla, T., Veselý, P.: WALTZ. http://kam.mff.cuni.cz/~vesely/tzaar/
12. Vasconcelos, P.: HsTZAAR. http://www.dcc.fc.up.pt/~pbv/stuff/hstzaar/
13. Veselý, P.: Artificial intelligence in abstract 2-player games. Bachelor's thesis, Faculty of Mathematics and Physics, Charles University in Prague, Czech Republic. http://kam.mff.cuni.cz/~vesely/tzaar/thesis.pdf (2012)
14. Wentink, D.: Analysis and implementation of the game Gipf. Master's thesis, Universiteit Maastricht (2001)
15. Winands, M.H.M., Schadd, M.P.D.: Evaluation-function based proof-number search. In: van den Herik, H.J., Iida, H., Plaat, A. (eds.) CG 2010. LNCS, vol. 6515, pp. 23–35. Springer, Heidelberg (2011)
16. Wu, I.-C., Lin, H.-H., Lin, P.-H., Sun, D.-J., Chan, Y.-C., Chen, B.-T.: Job-level proof-number search for Connect6. In: van den Herik, H.J., Iida, H., Plaat, A. (eds.) CG 2010. LNCS, vol. 6515, pp. 11–22. Springer, Heidelberg (2011). http://dl.acm.org/citation.cfm?id=1950322.1950324
17. Yoshizoe, K.: A new proof-number calculation technique for proof-number search. In: van den Herik, H.J., Xu, X., Ma, Z., Winands, M.H.M. (eds.) CG 2008. LNCS, vol. 5131, pp. 135–145. Springer, Heidelberg (2008)

18. Boiteajeux board-gaming portal. http://www.boiteajeux.net/
19. GAMES game awards. Games Magazine. http://www.gamesmagazine-online.com/
    gameslinks/archives.html2009awards
20. List of games, ICGA tournaments. [cit. 2013-05-11]. http://www.grappa.
    univ-lille3.fr/icga/games.php
21. Spiel des jahres, awarded games 2008. http://www.spiel-des-jahres.com/cms/
    front_content.php?idart=925
22. Tzaar - ai game project for 2011. http://www.math.uaa.alaska.edu/~afkjm/cs405/
    tzaar/

Perfectly Solving Domineering Boards

Jos W.H.M. Uiterwijk[✉]

Department of Knowledge Engineering (DKE), Maastricht University,
Maastricht, The Netherlands
uiterwijk@maastrichtuniversity.nl

Abstract. In this paper we describe the perfect solving of rectangular empty Domineering boards. *Perfect solving* is defined as solving without any search. This is done solely based on the number of various move types in the initial position. For this purpose we first characterize several such move types. Next we define 12 knowledge rules, of increasing complexity. Of these rules, 6 can be used to show that the starting player (assumed to be Vertical) can win a game against any opposition, while 6 can be used to prove a definite loss (a win for the second player, Horizontal).

Applying this knowledge-based method to all 81 rectangular boards up to 10 × 10 (omitting the trivial 1 × n and m × 1 boards), 67 could be solved perfectly. This is in sharp contrast with previous publications reporting the solution of Domineering boards, where only a few tiny boards were solved perfectly, the remainder requiring up to large amounts of search. Applying this method to larger boards with one or both sizes up to 30 solves 216 more boards, mainly with one dimension odd. All results fully agree with previously reported game-theoretic values.

Finally, we prove some more general theorems: (1) all m × 3 boards (m > 1) are a win for Vertical; (2) all 2k × n boards with n = 3, 5, 7, 9, and 11 are a win for Vertical; (3) all 3 × n boards (n > 3) are a win for Horizontal; and (4) all m × 2k boards for m = 5 and 9, all m × 2k boards with k > 1 for m = 3 and 7, and all 11 × 4k boards are a win for Horizontal.

1 Introduction

Domineering is a two-player perfect-information game invented by Göran Andersson around 1973. It was popularized to the general public in an article by Martin Gardner [9]. It can be played on any subset of a square lattice, though mostly it is restricted to rectangular m × n boards, where m denotes the number of rows and n the number of columns. The version introduced by Andersson and Gardner was the 8 × 8 board.

Play consists of the two players alternately placing a 1 × 2 tile (domino) on the board, where the first player may place the tile only in a vertical alignment, the second player only horizontally. Dominoes may not overlap. The first player being unable to move loses the game, his opponent (who made the last move) being declared the winner. Since the board is gradually filled, i.e., Domineering is a converging game, the game always ends, and ties are impossible. With these

T. Cazenave et al. (Eds.): CGW 2013, CCIS 408, pp. 97–121, 2014.
DOI: 10.1007/978-3-319-05428-5_8, © Springer International Publishing Switzerland 2014

rules the game belongs to the category of *combinatorial games*, for which a whole theory (the Combinatorial Game Theory) has been developed, especially by Conway [8] and Berlekamp et al. in their famous book set *Winning Ways* [3]. In combinatorial game theory the first player conventionally is called Left, the second Right, though in our case we will use the more convenient indications of Vertical and Horizontal, for the first and second player, respectively.

Among combinatorial game theorists Domineering received quite some attention, but this was limited to rather small or irregular boards [1–3,8,11,16]. Larger (rectangular) boards were solved using $\alpha\beta$ search [12], leading to solving all boards up to and including the standard 8×8 board [4], later extended to the 9×9 board [10], and finally extended to larger boards up to 10×10 [5,6].

2   Characteristics of Domineering

The knowledge rules to be defined in Sect. 3 are based on (counts for) several types of moves. These are defined here. We then define some parameters counting these move types. The move types and parameters will be illustrated for the 4×4 board. Next we will give some characteristics of the moves.

2.1   Move Types

We characterize moves in Domineering based on their vulnerability (can a move be prevented by the opponent?) and their destructive power (how many moves of the opponent are prevented by the move?). This leads to the following types of moves.

– A *destroyable* move is a move that can be prevented by the opponent, if it is his turn to move.
– A *safe* move is a move that cannot be prevented by the opponent (both squares are unreachable for him).
– A *double-destroying* (or *DD* for short) move is a move that diminishes the number of *real moves* of the opponent (the maximum number of moves the opponent would be able to put on the current board if he was allowed to do so; see Sect. 2.2 for a more formal definition) by 2. Therefore, each square of the DD move should prevent a move of the opponent separately.
– Analogously, a *single-destroying* (*SD*) move is a move that diminishes the number of real moves of the opponent by 1. Therefore, only one of the two squares of the SD move should prevent a move of the opponent.
– A *zero-destroying* (*ZD*) move is a move that does not diminish the number of real moves of the opponent.
– An *extended double-destroying* (*xDD*) move is a move that diminishes the number of DD moves of the opponent by 2. Therefore, both squares of the DD move should prevent a DD move of the opponent. These are under specific circumstances (see Lemma 5) the most powerful moves.

- A *safe-making* (*SM*) move is a move that increases the number of safe moves of the current player. According to the number of safe moves created they can be categorized further as being of type 1 (SM1) or 2 (SM2) for generating 1 or 2 additional safe moves.
- An *extended safe-making* (*xSM*) move is a SM move that is created by a SM move, not overlapping another SM move.

2.2 Board Parameters

Next we use parameters counting the numbers of some move types.

- $RealCur$ = number of real moves of the current player, which is the maximum number of moves the current player can put on the board if the opponent does not move further. Note that this is not the number of possible moves by the player, since possible moves can overlap.
- $DDCur$ = maximum number of DD moves the current player can put on the board if the opponent does not move further. Again, this is not the number of possible DD moves, since after playing a DD move other moves may change their nature.
- $xDDCur$ = maximum number of xDD moves the current player can put on the board if the opponent does not move further.
- $SafeCur$ = number of non-overlapping safe moves the current player has on the board.
- $SM1Cur$, $SM2Cur$, and $xSMCur$ = number of non-overlapping SM moves of types 1, 2, and extended, the current player can put on the board.

The $RealCur$ and $SafeCur$ parameters were already used by Breuker *et al.* [4,14] and Bullock [5,6] in their programs DOMI and OBSEQUI, respectively. The analogous parameters $RealOpp$, $DDOpp$, $xDDOpp$, $SafeOpp$, $SM1Opp$, $SM2Opp$, and $xSMOpp$, are defined similarly for the opponent. Note that the parameters for the opponent are counts as if the opponent were to move, i.e., neglecting effects of the move the current player can make.

Let us illustrate these move types and parameters with an example, to be used throughout this and the next section. For the 4×4 board (see Fig. 1a), Vertical has 12 possible moves (3 per column), of which maximally 8 can be put on the empty board ($RealCur = 8$). Moreover, every move of Vertical is a DD move on the empty board, however it is taken into account that DD moves may change the nature of future moves. E.g., a move like 1 in Fig. 1b will change the future move 5 in Fig. 1d from DD to non-DD (in this case into a safe move). For the empty 4×4 board the maximum number of DD moves Vertical can put on the board is 4, so $DDCur = 4$. Vertical has four xDD moves (all moves covering the 2nd and 3rd square of each column, though again maximally two can be put on the board ($xDDCur = 2$). Of course, Vertical has no safe moves on the empty board yet ($SafeCur = 0$). However, every move in the 2nd or 3rd column generates a safe move of type 1, so $SM1Cur = 4$. Other SM counts are 0 for this example, in particular $xSMCur = 0$, since extended SM moves

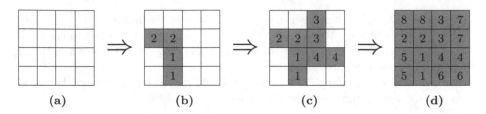

Fig. 1. A possible (non-optimal) move sequence on the 4 × 4 board.

may not overlap with SM moves. Note that for the 4 × 4 board all analogous opponent parameters have the same values as their counterparts for the current player. This holds for any empty square board. For non-square boards analogous parameters may have different values.

We also introduce a notation for Domineering games. We use a chess-like notation for boards, where columns are denoted from left to right with 'a', 'b', etc, and rows from bottom to top by '1', '2', etc. A square is denoted by its column and row. So, for the 4 × 4 board the four corner squares starting in the left-down corner are denoted by 'a1', 'a4', 'd4', and 'd1', in clockwise order. A vertical move is indicated by the lower square of the domino, for a horizontal move we indicate the left square of the domino. Unlike Chess, we use a separate move number for each move separately, so that all odd-numbered moves are moves made by Vertical (the first player) and all even-numbered moves are moves made by Horizontal (the second player). In this notation we denote the move sequence in Fig. 1 by **1. b1 2. a3 3. c3 4. c2 5. a1 6. c1 7. d3 8. a4 0-1** (Horizontal wins).

2.3   Move-Type Characteristics

In this section we describe some characteristics of move types, that are important for the knowledge rules to be defined in the next section. Formal proofs are by careful case analysis, but are omitted here for space reasons.

Lemma 1. *Every DD move is destroyable*

On empty boards, the number of DD moves is given by the number of non-overlapping empty 2 × 2 regions on the board (quadrants). If the dimension of the board is even in the opponent's direction, any move of the current player on an empty board is a DD move, if it is odd, only moves in the even columns (for Vertical) or rows (for Horizontal) are DD moves. If both dimensions are odd, only moves covering the (even, even) squares are DD moves. So, for an empty $m \times n$ board $DDCur = DDOpp = \lfloor \frac{m}{2} \rfloor \times \lfloor \frac{n}{2} \rfloor$. By their nature of covering essential squares in quadrants, a DD move by a player can always be destroyed by his opponent. So a DD move is both aggressive and vulnerable.

Lemma 2. *DD moves destroy each other in pairs*

In every empty quadrant, Vertical to move can destroy one horizontal DD move (and one non-DD move) using a DD move, and vice versa. Consequently, as long as only DD moves are played (in the first phase of the game) it holds that $DDCur = DDOpp$.

Lemma 3. *Two DD moves can be destroyed in one move only with an xDD move*

An xDD move is a move involving 2 quadrants, deleting one opponent DD move in each, at the cost of also using 2 DD moves. This is only possible when the size of the board in that direction is even. An example of an xDD move is move 1 in Fig. 2a.

Lemma 4. *Every SM move is also a DD move*

Since a SM move together with the safe move generated (making these squares inaccessible for the opponent) cover a whole quadrant, every SM move destroys two opponent moves, hence is a DD move.

Lemma 5. *An xDD move is only profitable on even by even boards when the number of DD moves is even*

Since using an xDD move is at the cost of one additional move (diminishing $RealCur$ by 2) and possibly at the cost of one safe move generated (if a safe move is generated, using it would cost again an additional move), playing an xDD move should only be applied when the number of DD moves is even and the opponent can not reply with an xDD move, since then the player to move effectively can use one DD move more than the opponent. Even then playing xDD moves may not be useful. However, when the size of the board in the opponent's direction is also even, an additional advantage of using an xDD move is that such a move guarantees two additional opponent moves to be destroyable. Consequently, an xDD move if possible should only be applied on even × even boards when the number of DD moves is even and the opponent cannot respond with an xDD move.

To show that using an xDD move is profitable in and only in this case, we provide the following proof.

Proof. Suppose that Vertical has the possibility to play the last xDD move. Consider the position in the game at which the number of DD moves left is exactly 2, and arbitrarily assume that Vertical is able to use his xDD move at this position. Let i and j be the number of real moves of Vertical and Horizontal, respectively, at this point in the game. We use the notation $\bar{i}/j$ for the number of i vertical and j horizontal moves in a position, the overline indicating the player to move. Then if Vertical would not use his xDD move, but in stead plays a regular DD move, Horizontal might respond by playing the last DD move. So in this case play might proceed as $\bar{i}/j \Rightarrow i{-}1/\overline{j{-}2} \Rightarrow \overline{i{-}3}/j{-}3 \Rightarrow i{-}4/\overline{j{-}3} \Rightarrow \overline{i{-}5}/j{-}4 \Rightarrow i{-}6/\overline{j{-}4}$.

Here we have given three additional moves from the position where the DD moves are exhausted, assuming pessimistically that the opponent (Horizontal) always can destroy a (single) vertical move, whereas Vertical cannot destroy an opponent move. Using the xDD move on the other hand leads to the following sequence: $\overline{i}/j \Rightarrow i-2/\overline{j-2} \Rightarrow \overline{i-3}/j-3 \Rightarrow i-4/\overline{j-3} \Rightarrow \overline{i-5}/j-4 \Rightarrow i-6/\overline{j-4}$. Clearly there is no net gain. If, however, Vertical also takes advantage of the possibility to destroy an additional move in this phase of the game, the sequence would be $\overline{i}/j \Rightarrow i-2/\overline{j-2} \Rightarrow \overline{i-3}/j-3 \Rightarrow i-4/\overline{j-4}$. So, for the same reduction in number of opponent moves Vertical has consumed 2 moves less. Note that even when using an xDD move is at the cost of a SM move, the player using the xDD move still will have a profit of 1. $\square$

The profitable use of an xDD move is captured in the level-6 rules (see Sect. 3.6) and exemplified by Fig. 2.

Lemma 6. *More destructive moves are always better than less destructive moves*

Due to the nature of the game a player should always destroy as many moves of the opponent as possible in every position. In particular, both players will play DD moves as long as available (phase 1 of the game). After that, SD moves will be used as long as available to at least one player (phase 2 of the game). Only then both players will use ZD moves till the end of the game (phase 3).

3   Perfectly Solving Domineering

In this section we report on *perfectly solving* Domineering positions, which we define as solving without any search, i.e., completely knowledge-based. For this purpose, we have defined 6 sets of knowledge rules of increasing difficulty level (and power) to prove for a position that the first or second player can always win. The rules are based on the fact that for a player it is always better to play a move of larger destructive power than of lower destructive power (see Lemma 6), if known, and depend solely on the number and types of moves defined in the previous section. They do not take specific locations of moves into account (which would imply a covert form of searching). Every set consists of a pair of (dual) rules, the first one testing a first-player's win potential, the second rule testing the second player's win potential. Note that the rules are not complementary, but cumulative, thus incorporating the full power of the rules of lower level.

3.1   Level-1 Rules

A position is a win for the current player if $RealCur > RealOpp$ **and** $SafeCur \geq RealOpp$. This is evident: if after playing an arbitrary move the current player has as many safe moves as real moves of the opponent, the current player is guaranteed to make the last move.

Alternately, a position is a win for the opponent (so a loss for the current player) if $SafeOpp \geq RealCur$. Here the opponent needs at least as many safe moves as the current player has real moves, but not necessarily more moves. This is a consequence of the fact that it is the current player's obligation to move (called the *combinatorial advantage* of the second player).

3.2   Level-2 Rules

The level-1 rules can be enhanced by realizing that an opponent move can maximally destroy two moves of the current player, after which the current player has to play a (third) move, possibly destroying none of the opponent's moves. This means that the current player needs maximally 3 times the number of real moves of the opponent. In addition, any safe move of the current player counts for one move of the opponent (safe moves cannot be destroyed). This leads to the following two rules. (1) A position is a win for the current player if $RealCur > 3 \times RealOpp - 2 \times SafeCur$, and (2) a position is a loss for the current player if $RealOpp \geq 3 \times RealCur - 2 \times SafeOpp$.

For the 4×4 board this means that Vertical ("having to move first") would need at least 25 real moves to have a guaranteed win, whereas Horizontal would need 24 real moves.

However, these rules can be enhanced considerably, by realizing that at every turn of the current player he can at least transform a DD move of the opponent if any into a SD move, or otherwise a SD move into a ZD move, again if any. Moreover, the above formulae assume that all opponent moves are of type DD, which they are not. This leads to new formulae, that are quite complex and include notions of the effective number of DD moves, the effective number of SD moves, etc. It is much easier (and less error-prone) to implement a function that just calculates the number of real moves a player needs to win the game (called the *threshold*). This function has as input $RealOpp$, $DDOpp$, and $SafeCur$ for testing a vertical win, and $RealCur$, $DDCur$, and $SafeOpp$ for testing a horizontal win. The function simulates the move type sequence, assuming optimal move decisions for both players (the opponent playing DD moves, as long as available, playing SD moves if available otherwise, and the current player transforming an opponent DD move into an SD move if possible, otherwise transforming an opponent SD move into a ZD move, if possible). We call such a sequence the *optimal move-type sequence* (OMTS) and the associated function the $OMTS_k\text{-}P$ function. The subscript k indicates the knowledge-rules' level and P can be V or H standing for a win test for Vertical or Horizontal, respectively.

For the 4×4 board, the OMTS sequence is as follows.

8(4,4)	8(3,5)*	7(2,5)	7(1,6)*	6(0,6)	6(0,5)*	5(0,4)	5(0,3)*	4(0,2)	4(0,1)*	...
16/0*	15/0	13/0*	12/0	10/0*	9/0	8/0*	7/0	6/0*	5/0	...

...	3(0,0)	3(0,0)*	2(0,0)	2(0,0)*	1(0,0)	1(0,0)*	0(0,0)	0(0,0)*
...	4/0*	3/0	3/0*	2/0	2/0*	1/0	1/0*	0/0

Above the horizontal line are the opponent moves, in the form $RealOpp(DDOpp, SDOpp)$. Remaining opponent moves are assumed to be of type ZD ($ZDOpp =$

RealOpp − *DDOpp* − *SDOpp*). To guarantee correctness of the rule we always assume maximum power of the opponent initially, in particular that all non-DD moves of the opponent are SD moves. Below the horizontal line are the corresponding current player's moves, in the form *RealCur*/*SafeCur*. A '*' denotes the player to move. It should be read by starting at the opponent's initial configuration (above, left) and "playing" until the opponent loses, indicated by the $0(0,0)$* (the opponent is to move and has no more moves left). In this line, if the opponent is to move the next entry has 1 *RealOpp* less, playing a double-destroying move if possible, otherwise a single-destroying move if possible. If it is the current player's turn, the opponent's potential is decreased by 1 (transforming a DD move into a SD move if possible, otherwise a SD move into a ZD move if possible). No opponent move is destroyed according to the rules at this level. After reaching the loss condition for the opponent (upper line, right), the needed current player's moves are "constructed" (lower line, from right to left), terminating in the number of moves required to win. Here, if in the configuration the current player is to move, *RealCur* is augmented by one, and if possible *SafeCur* also. Otherwise, the increase in *RealCur* is 0 when *RealCur* ≤ *SafeCur* (the player only has safe moves left), otherwise the increment depends on the available opponent moves here (entry above): 2 if DD moves are available, otherwise 1 if SD moves are available, else 0.

The given example shows that if *RealOpp* = 8, *DDOpp* = 4, and *SafeCur* = 0, $OMTS_2$-$V(8,4,0) = 16$, meaning that 16 real moves for Vertical assure him the win, a deficit of 8 compared to *RealCur*.

The equivalent loss-rule is similar, by assuming that at the start board Horizontal just moved (a kind of "null" move), after which Vertical has the opponent role and Horizontal acts as current player. Since $OMTS_2$-$H(8,4,0) = 15$ it follows that Horizontal needs 15 moves to win the game, a deficit of 7.

3.3   Level-3 Rules

The level-3 rules are an easy yet powerful improvement upon the level-2 rules, by realizing that any DD move of the opponent is destroyable (see Lemma 1). Therefore, as long as the opponent has DD moves left, the current player always will destroy 1 of these per move.

For the 4×4 example, realizing that Vertical can delete a horizontal DD move twice, gives an $OMTS_3$-$V(8,4,0)$ threshold of 13, a gain of 3 compared with the level-2 rules, but still a deficit of 5 (see the following OMTS sequence).

8(4,4)	7(3,4)*	6(2,4)	5(1,4)*	4(0,4)	4(0,3)*	3(0,2)	3(0,1)*	2(0,0)	2(0,0)*	1(0,0)	...
13/0*	12/0	10/0*	9/0	7/0*	6/0	5/0*	4/0	3/0*	2/0	2/0*	...

...	1(0,0)*	0(0,0)	0(0,0)*
...	1/0	1/0*	0/0

The corresponding loss condition is given by $OMTS_3$-$H(8,4,0) = 12$, also a gain of 3, and a deficit of 4 now.

3.4   Level-4 Rules

At this level, the evaluator explicitly takes into account the number of DD moves of the current player also. As long as available, the current player will play a DD move, deleting 2 moves of the opponent per own move. It can be shown for empty boards (see Lemma 2) that among these two moves deleted from the opponent always 1 can be a DD move, as long as available. This means that, as long as both players have DD moves, they will alternate playing them, always deleting 2 moves of the other player, including 1 DD move. Effectively this means that per iteration (1 DD move by both players) the count of real moves of both players diminishes by 3, and the number of DD moves by 2. One additional requirement to guarantee correctness of the V-win rule is that if, after Vertical's first move, an even number of DD moves is left, Horizontal will play if possible an xDD move once (the only way to diminish the opponent's number of DD moves by 2, see Lemma 3). We do not take into account possible disadvantages for Horizontal (i.e., we just assume maximal usefulness for the opponent). Similarly, for correctness of the H-win rule Vertical plays as first move an xDD move, if available, when the number of DD moves is even.

For the 4×4 example, the corresponding OMTS$_4$-V(8,4,0) call yields a threshold of 10, a gain of 3 compared with the level-3 rules, but still a deficit of 2. This is shown in the following OMTS sequence.

8(4,4)	6(3,3)*	5(2,3)	3(1,2)*	2(0,2)	2(0,1)*	1(0,0)	1(0,0)*	0(0,0)	0(0,0)*
10/0*	9/0	7/0*	6/0	4/0*	3/0	2/0*	1/0	1/0*	0/0

Note that we do not need to supply the $DDCur$ parameter, since $DDCur$ is always equal to $DDOpp$. In the present case, no xDD move is used by the opponent (Horizontal), since when it is his turn the number of DD moves left is odd.

Trying to prove that Horizontal can win gives OMTS$_4$-H(8,4,0) = 10, also a deficit of 2. Here, Vertical is allowed an xDD move once, since at his turn the number of DD moves is even.

3.5   Level-5 Rules

One further important enhancement is to recognize how many safe moves the current player minimally will achieve. A safe move is generated by a SM move, which only can be used in the first phase, when both players only use DD moves (see Lemma 4). The building of safe moves is essential in bringing the thresholds down further, since in the last stage of the move sequence any opponent move then just requires 1 current player's move. This is either the case when the opponent only has ZD moves left, and/or when the current player has only safe moves left.

In order to recognize how many safe moves the current player can build, we first determine the number and types of the SM moves. A SM move generates 1 safe move at a time (in the 2nd or $(n-1)^{th}$ column for Vertical, and equivalently in the 2nd or $(m-1)^{th}$ row for Horizontal, or 2 safe moves for $m \times 3$ boards for Vertical, and $3 \times n$ boards for Horizontal. Further, we calculate how many of the type-1 SM moves generate themselves new SM moves (the number of xSM moves). We then calculate the effective number of safe moves the current player will create during the first phase of the move sequence (effectively by counting every odd move of the series with SM moves plus xSM moves generated) and add this number to $SafeCur$. For Horizontal, the corresponding number is given by counting the even moves of the corresponding series.

For the 4×4 example, realizing that Vertical has 4 SM moves, of which he can use at least 2, and no xSM moves, the number of safe moves of the current player is augmented by 2, giving an $OMTS_5$-$V(8,4,2)$ threshold of 9, a gain of 1 compared with the level-4 rule, but still lacking a single move (see the next OMTS sequence).

8(4,4)	6(3,3)*	5(2,3)	3(1,2)*	2(0,2)	2(0,1)*	1(0,0)	1(0,0)*	0(0,0)	0(0,0)*
9/2*	8/2	6/2*	5/2	3/2*	2/2	2/2*	1/1	1/1*	0/0

Trying to prove a Horizontal win does not make any progress, since $OMTS_5$-$H(8,4,2)$ still has a value of 10.

3.6   Level-6 Rules

On level 6 we take the availability of xDD moves fully into account. This means that if a player with an even number of DD moves left among which is at least an xDD move, and if both dimensions of the board are even, he will use that one, on the additional condition that the opponent can not (anymore) respond with an xDD move himself (see Lemma 5). Essential is that an xDD move makes two non-DD opponent moves destroyable, at the cost of not using one safe move generated. Playing an xDD move should only be done when profitable to the player to move. The determination which player can effectively use the last xDD move (denoted as having the *xDD-lead*), if any, requires careful analysis and is the most difficult component of the knowledge rules so far. It presently has been determined for all even $\times$ even boards with sizes up to 10. Moreover, it can easily be shown that for $m \times n$ boards with $n = 2, 4$, and 6 and m even and ≥ 10 (all being extended in the vertical direction) Vertical has the xDD-lead, whereas similarly for the horizontally extended boards ($m \times n$ boards with $m = 2, 4$, and 6 and n even and ≥ 10) Horizontal has the xDD-lead.

For the 4×4 example, Vertical indeed can better play an xDD move. We decrement the number of safe moves that Vertical can obtain by 1 (for the xDD move used), and we take into account that 2 opponent moves left are destroyable. This gives an $OMTS_6$-$V(8,4,1)$ threshold of 8, which is just enough to guarantee Vertical the win.

8(4,4)	6(2,4)*	5(1,4)	3(0,3)*	2(0,2)	1(0,1)*	0(0,0)	0(0,0)*
8/1*	6/1	4/1*	3/1	2/1*	1/1	1/1*	0/0

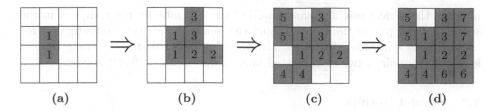

Fig. 2. An optimal move sequence on the 4×4 board.

The corresponding Horizontal-win test, though not relevant anymore, would give $\mathrm{OMTS}_6\text{-}H(8,4,2) = 9$, still 1 deficit.

To show the profitable use of an xDD move in practise, we give in Fig. 2 an optimal move sequence for the 4×4 board.

Here, Vertical plays an xDD move right at the start (move **1**), after which Horizontal is unable to respond with an xDD move himself. In this way Vertical effectively can use one DD move more than Horizontal (2 against 1 instead of 2 against 2 when no xDD move is played). The first phase ends after move **3** (see Fig. 2b). Moreover, Vertical is guaranteed to be able to play a SD move in the second phase of the game (move **5** in Fig. 2c). In the final phase, both players just play their supply of safe moves (Fig. 2d), after which Horizontal is the first player being unable to move. So by the profitable use of the xDD move Vertical assures the win, even though the use of the xDD move was at the cost of a safe move generated (1 in stead of 2, cf. Fig. 1).

4   Results

For testing our rules we used the set of all rectangular empty $m \times n$ boards, m and n both ranging from 2–10. These are more or less the same boards as solved by OBSEQUI [5,6]. For all boards Vertical is the first player. Of course an $m \times n$ board with Vertical to move is equivalent with an $n \times m$ board with Horizontal to move. All tests are done in increasing level of the rule set in use.

4.1   Level-1 and Level-2 Results

No boards are solved using these simple rule sets. The reason is obvious: for the level-1 and level-2 rules to be of any use we need at least some safe moves, which clearly is not the case for empty boards.

4.2   Level-3 Results

Incorporating the knowledge that every opponent DD move is destroyable solves 5 boards, all with one of the board dimensions equal to 3 and the other even. Though the results of these boards are rather obvious when inspecting them, we stress that the publications reporting on solved Domineering boards did not mention the perfect solving of any board of these. (Data are not complete in the sense that the publications only report the sums of the nodes investigated for $m \times n$ and $n \times m$ boards together, always being larger than 2, meaning that at least never a pair of two such related boards were both perfectly solved.)

4.3   Level-4 Results

The biggest step in number of perfectly solved boards is reached at level 4, when the DD moves of the current player are being used to their full potential (deleting 2 moves of the opponent, among which 1 DD move if available). This enhancement gives rise to 34 new boards perfectly solved. The newly solved boards include all boards of the shape $2k \times n$, with $n = 3, 5$ or 7, not yet solved at level 3. In Sect. 6 we will prove that such boards are always wins for Vertical (Theorems 1 and 2). They rely on the fact that Vertical has an initial advantage (by the fact that the width of the board is odd, whereas the height is even). Similarly, many of the $m \times 2k$ boards for $m = 3, 5, 7$, and 9 are proven to be horizontal wins, which also will lead to a generalization in Sect. 6 (Theorems 3 and 4).

4.4   Level-5 Results

Including the information on the number of safe moves guaranteed for the current player solves 13 more boards, including all 5 of the shape $2k \times 9$. Here, Vertical is able to build a sufficient potential of safe moves needed after both players' DD moves have been exhausted. In Sect. 6 we will prove that such boards also are always wins for Vertical.

4.5   Level-6 Results

Making full use of the xDD moves perfectly solves 15 more boards, 12 wins for Vertical, 3 for Horizontal. All of them are boards with both dimensions even, which makes sense, since it is one of the requirements for profitably using xDD moves.

4.6   Summary of Results up to 10 × 10

In Table 1 we summarize our results for boards up to 10×10. The table shows that 67 of the 81 boards are perfectly solved. Of these, 41 are wins for Vertical (61 %), and 26 for Horizontal (39 %). This indicates that like in many board games the first player has the advantage of the initiative (for a more general discussion of this phenomenon, see [14]). Realizing that Domineering, by virtue of being a combinatorial game, has an implicit advantage for the second player (since the last mover wins), we conclude that the advantage

Table 1. Summary of number of solutions for boards up to 10 × 10. The first and second columns give the level and the total number of solutions found for that level, distinguished into wins for Vertical (third column) and for Horizontal (fourth column). The last line gives the total counts.

level	sol.	V wins	H wins
1	0	0	0
2	0	0	0
3	5	3	2
4	34	18	16
5	13	8	5
6	15	12	3
total	67	41	26

Table 2. Summary of number of solutions for boards up to 30 × 30. Again, the first and second columns give the level and the total number of solutions found for that level, distinguished into the wins for Vertical (third column) and for Horizontal (fourth column). The last line gives the total counts.

level	sol.	V wins	H wins
1	0	0	0
2	0	0	0
3	15	8	7
4	137	67	70
5	76	50	26
6	55	37	18
total	283	162	121

of the initiative is quite large, outperforming the first player's combinatorial disadvantage.

4.7   Summary of Results up to 30 × 30

Given the success for boards up to 10 × 10 we decided to apply our method to all boards with sizes up to 30, again omitting the trivial 1 × n and m × 1 boards. The results are summarized in Table 2. For all unsolved boards for which no xDD analysis was performed (the even × even boards with both dimensions ≥ 8, except 8 × 8, 8 × 10, 10 × 8, and 10 × 10), we tried the possibilities that Vertical, Horizontal, or none of the players has the xDD-lead. None of these possibilities led to additionally solved boards, which means that the results in the table are complete up to 30 × 30, also for level 6.

The table shows that 283 of the 841 boards are perfectly solved. Of these, 162 are wins for Vertical (57 %), and 121 for Horizontal (43 %). We see that the percentage of vertical wins is diminished compared to the smaller test set, which indicates that the advantage of the initiative is especially notable for smaller boards, a phenomenon also observed for other games [10,14].

5   Discussion

In this section we will discuss the results and provide arguments for the correctness of the methods applied. Also we will sketch a winning strategy for won positions, based on the knowledge rules used to solve the games.

5.1   Discussion of Results

An overview of all perfectly solved rectangular boards with dimensions from 2 to 10 is given in Table 3. For solved boards the minimum level needed for solving is indicated. For unsolved boards, we provide the *deficits* for Vertical and Horizontal (i.e., the differences between the number of moves guaranteeing a win and the real number of moves, according to the level-6 rules).

Table 3. Game-theoretic values of many $m \times n$ Domineering boards, for $m, n \leq 10$, Vertical moving first. V indicates a Vertical win, H a Horizontal win. The subscript indicates the lowest knowledge level able to perfectly solve the board. For non-solved boards an entry m/n gives the deficits for Vertical/Horizontal at level 6, the overline indicating the winning side, according to previously published results.

$m\backslash n$	2	3	4	5	6	7	8	9	10
2	V_4	V_3	H_5	V_4	V_6	V_4	H_5	V_5	V_6
3	V_5	V_4	H_3	H_4	H_4	$3/\overline{1}$	H_3	H_4	H_4
4	V_6	V_4	V_6	V_4	V_6	V_4	H_6	V_5	H_6
5	H_4	V_5	H_4	$3/\overline{2}$	H_4	$5/\overline{1}$	H_4	H_5	H_4
6	V_4	V_3	V_6	V_4	V_6	V_4	H_6	V_5	$\overline{2}/2$
7	V_5	V_4	H_4	$\overline{2}/4$	H_5	$\overline{1}/6$	H_4	$7/\overline{2}$	H_5
8	V_6	V_4	V_6	V_4	V_6	V_4	$\overline{1}/3$	V_5	$4/\overline{3}$
9	H_4	V_4	H_4	$\overline{1}/6$	H_4	$\overline{3}/6$	H_4	$\overline{6}/6$	H_4
10	V_4	V_3	V_6	V_4	V_6	V_4	$\overline{2}/5$	V_5	$\overline{3}/8$

Some observations are in order. (1) All results are fully in agreement with previously published results (see, e.g., [7]). (2) The smallest board not solved is 3×7. A closer inspection shows that to solve this board rules are needed that guarantee a player the ability to destroy opponent moves in the second phase of the game, something that is lacking in the present rule set, apart from the small use in level 6 after playing an xDD move. See also Sect. 8 on future research in this direction. (3) The next-smallest board not solved is 5×5. This is indeed a difficult board, the only square board known to be a win for Horizontal. Moreover, this is the smallest of five non-solved square boards in the test set. This makes sense, since these boards are inherently difficult to solve (and play), since neither player has an explicit starting advantage in number of real moves, and the advantage of the initiative of the first player is more or less balanced by the combinatorial advantage of the second player, leading to rather even boards. (4) We observe that all odd × even and even × odd boards are solved. This also makes sense, since for these boards one of the players has a starting advantage

Table 4. Game-theoretic values of many perfectly solved $m \times n$ Domineering boards, for $m, n \leq 30$, Vertical moving first. V indicates a Vertical win, H a Horizontal win.

m\n	2	3	4	5	6	7	8	9	10	11	12	13	14	15	16	17	18	19	20	21	22	23	24	25	26	27	28	29	30
2	V	V	H	V	V	V	H	V	V	V	H			V	H			V	H				H				H		
3	V	V	H	H	H	H	H	H	H	H	H	H	H	H	H	H	H	H	H	H	H	H	H	H	H	H	H	H	H
4	V	V	V	V	V	V	H	V	H	V	H		H		H		H		H		H		H		H		H		H
5	H	V	H		H		H	H	H	H	H	H	H	H	H	H	H	H	H	H	H	H	H	H	H	H	H	H	H
6	V	V	V	V	V	V	H	V		V	H				H				H				H				H		
7	V	V	H		H		H		H		H	H	H	H	H	H	H	H	H	H	H	H	H	H	H	H	H	H	H
8	V	V	V	V	V	V		V		V																			
9	H	V	H		H		H		H		H		H		H		H		H		H		H		H		H		H
10	V	V	V	V	V	V		V		V																			
11	V	V	H	V		V	H				H				H				H				H				H		
12	V	V	V	V	V	V		V		V																			
13		V		V																									
14	V	V	V	V	V	V		V		V																			
15	V	V		V		V																							
16	V	V	V	V	V	V		V		V																			
17		V		V		V																							
18	V	V	V	V	V	V		V		V																			
19	V	V		V		V																							
20	V	V	V	V	V	V		V		V																			
21		V		V		V																							
22	V	V	V	V	V	V		V		V																			
23	V	V		V		V																							
24	V	V	V	V	V	V		V		V																			
25		V		V		V																							
26	V	V	V	V	V	V		V		V																			
27	V	V		V		V																							
28	V	V	V	V	V	V		V		V																			
29		V		V		V																							
30	V	V	V	V	V	V		V		V																			

in number of real moves. (5) Of the 14 unsolved boards investigated, 5 have a deficit of 1 for the winning side, 5 of 2, 3 of 3, and 1 of 6 (9 × 9). The large number of small deficits for the winning players indicate that the level-6 rules are in these cases very close to solving, whereas 9 × 9 apparently is still far from being solved.

An overview of all perfectly solved rectangular boards with dimensions from 2 to 30 is given in Table 4. Here we refrain from giving information on knowledge level or deficits.

The table shows that when the boards are vertically extended ($m > n$) Vertical has a clear advantage, especially when the number of columns is odd. Similarly, for horizontally extended boards ($m < n$) Horizontal has the advantage, especially when the number of rows is odd. An even closer inspection led to the formulation of four theorems (see Sect. 6) explaining these findings. We further remark that, although no boards have been solved of which the game-theoretic value was not known so far, several such boards have very low deficits (not given in Table 4 for space reasons), indicating that they are probably close to being solved. Again, see Sect. 8 on future research for more ideas in this direction.

An up-to-date overview of all known game-theoretic values of Domineering boards with sizes up to 30, including information on whether they are perfectly solved, solved by search or combinatorial game theory, or by using translational symmetry rules, is given in Appendix A.

5.2   Correctness of Results

Though the correctness of the results is difficult to be verified, we provide four arguments supporting the validity of the rules used and the correctness of their implementation.

1. All rules have been closely inspected and their results have elaborately been investigated by case analysis.
2. All results obtained are fully in agreement with known game-theoretic values, either obtained by search or by theoretical consideration (as on Nathan Bullock's website with updated game theoretic values of Domineering boards [7]).
3. The rules are always applied in the order of increasing level. Since the rules are cumulative (fully incorporate the knowledge of lower-level rules), the number of moves required to prove a win never may grow. Of course it also holds that as soon as a win is proved for one side, no rule ever may prove a win for the other side. Therefore, as an additional check, after a position was solved we still applied all rules not applied yet. In no case we observed an increase in number of moves required, nor a contradiction between the results.
4. Although Theorems 1–4 (see next section) were triggered by the results, they were proven on theoretical considerations only. Therefore, we see the fact that all experimental results are fully in agreement with the theorems as further support for the methods used.

5.3   Winning Strategy

Naturally the question comes up whether the rules perfectly solving boards lead to an inherent playing strategy for won positions. Although this is in principle impossible, since a playing strategy guaranteeing a win per definition requires a winning move after **every** opponent's reply in the game (i.e., a *solution tree*, which only can be obtained by full search), we still can give a general strategy.

We first note that such a strategy is only applicable to empty rectangular boards, since all rules apply only to such positions.

Next we note that an optimal game consists of three phases, which by analogy with chess praxis we may call the opening (phase 1), the middle game (phase 2), and the endgame (phase 3). In the *opening* both players only play DD moves. The winning player makes sure meanwhile using as many SM moves as possible.

Only when use of an xDD move is possible and profitable, the winning player will use it at a moment after which the opponent cannot reply with an xDD move anymore. Note that playing an xDD move earlier, after which the opponent might be able to respond with an xDD move by himself, even if the current player then might be able to use an additional xDD move, never is profitable for the winning player, since successive xDD moves give no net gain, whereas they might lead to a further reduction in the supply of safe moves built. When the DD moves are exhausted, we enter the *middle game*. (Only in some cases when the supply of safe moves built is sufficiently large, this phase is skipped.) In the middle game the opponent always is assumed to play moves that also delete a move of the winning player, whereas the winning player does not. (He might have SD moves, himself, but this is not guaranteed by the rules, except once after a xDD move is played by one of the players.) The only requirement in this phase is that the winning side plays moves that at least diminish the destructive power of the opponent's moves (from SD to ZD moves). When the winning player only has safe moves left (which is equivalent to the opponent having only ZD moves left), we enter the *endgame*. This phase of the game is trivial, since it just means playing arbitrary moves until the opponent is out of supply.

6   Some General Theorems

Triggered by the results shown in Table 4 we noticed several patterns. Closer investigation led to four general theorems. These and their proofs are given below. Since the theorems are explicitly stated for either Vertical or Horizontal, we will use *RealV* and *RealH* in stead of *RealCur* and *RealOpp*, and likewise for the other parameters.

Theorem 1. *All $m \times 3$ boards $(m > 1)$ are a win for Vertical*

Proof. For $m \leq 5$ the results are obtained from Table 3. For an $m \times 3$ board with $m \geq 6$ we have the following. Suppose Vertical plays his first move at the bottom of the 2nd column, creating 2 safe moves. Now $RealH = m - 2$. The best case for Horizontal is when $m - 2$ is a 4-fold + 3, since then Horizontal has 1 more DD move than Vertical + one additional row, with Horizontal to move. So suppose $m - 2 = 4k + 3$ for $k \geq 1$. Then $RealH = 4k + 3$. Since in every pair of empty rows both Vertical and Horizontal have 1 DD move, every group of 4 rows implies 1 iteration, in which Horizontal and Vertical both play a DD move, effectively diminishing the number of real moves of both sides by 3. So after k iterations, $RealH = k + 3$. Since every DD move by Vertical creates 2 additional safe moves, the total number of safe moves of Vertical after k iterations has been increased to $2k + 2$. Since $2k + 2 \geq k + 3$ for all $k \geq 1$, it follows that Vertical has at least as many safe moves left as all moves of Horizontal, implying that Vertical always wins.   □

Next we prove that Vertical wins all $2k \times n$ boards with $n = 3, 5, 7, 9$, and 11. Of course, for $n = 3$ this is already covered by Theorem 1. However, to see

Table 5. Relevant information in the proof of Theorem 2.

	$2k \times 3$ k even	$2k \times 5$	$2k \times 7$ k even	$2k \times 9$	$2k \times 11$ k even
At start					
$RealV$	$3k$	$5k$	$7k$	$9k$	$11k$
$RealH$	$2k$	$4k$	$6k$	$8k$	$10k$
DD	k	$2k$	$3k$	$4k$	$5k$
# iter. 1st phase	$1/2k$	k	$1^1/2k$	$2k$	$2^1/2k$
After 1st phase					
$RealV$	$1^1/2k$	$2k$	$2^1/2k$	$3k$	$3^1/2k$
$RealH$	$1/2k$	k	$1^1/2k$	$2k$	$2^1/2k$
$SafeV$	k	k	$1^1/2k + 1$	$\lfloor 1^1/2k \rfloor + 1$	$1^1/2k + 1$
# iter. 3rd phase	$1/2k$	k	$1^1/2k$	$\lfloor 1^1/2k \rfloor + 1$	$1^1/2k + 1$
Remainder for 2nd phase					
$RealV$	$k - 1$	$k - 1$	$k - 1$	$\lceil 1^1/2k \rceil - 2$	$2k - 2$
$RealH$	0	0	0	$\lceil 1/2k \rceil - 1$	$k - 1$

the pattern in this method more clearly, we include the case $n = 3$ in the next theorem also.

Theorem 2. *All* $2k \times n$ *boards for* $n = 3, 5, 7, 9,$ *and* 11 *are a win for Vertical*

Proof. We start by giving relevant information in Table 5.

The first block (at the top) gives the number of real moves of Vertical and Horizontal, and the number of DD moves, at the start, for the five cases $2k \times 3$, $2k \times 5$, $2k \times 7$, $2k \times 9$, and $2k \times 11$. For the cases $2k \times 3$, $2k \times 7$, and $2k \times 11$ we first consider the case with k is even. In the first phase of the game both players will play their DD moves. No xDD moves will be played due to the fact that the width of the board is odd. The length of this phase is half the number of DD moves, so $1/2k$, k, $1^1/2k$, $2k$, and $2^1/2k$ iterations, respectively (see next row). During this phase, every iteration reduces $RealV$ and $RealH$ both with 3. Note that for these five cases the number of DD moves is always even, so it is always Vertical's move after the first phase.

The values of $RealV$ and $RealH$ after this phase, together with $SafeV$, the number of safe moves built by Vertical, are given in the second block. Note that for $2k \times 3$ boards, k safe moves have been generated after $1/2k$ iterations, due to the fact that all SM moves are of type 2. For $2k \times 5$ boards k iterations generate k safe moves, since all vertical DD moves are SM moves of type 1 (no xSM moves). For the $2k \times n$ boards with $n = 7, 9,$ and 11 the $1^1/2k$, $2k$, and $2^1/2k$ iterations in this phase generate $\lfloor 1^1/2k \rfloor + 1$ safe moves, since this is the maximum number of safe moves guaranteed after the first phase (from $2k$ SM moves of type 1 and $2k$ extended SM moves). The additional safe move results from the fact that the first move on a $2k \times n$ board for $n \geq 7$ transforms an xSM move into an SM move and adds another xSM move, yielding one additional safe move.

In the last phase of the game, Vertical will play these safe moves, each against a single move of Horizontal. Since we let Vertical start this phase also, Vertical needs at least one more move. This phase lasts until Horizontal has no more moves left, or Vertical has used his full supply of safe moves, i.e., the minimum of $RealH$ and $SafeV$ in the second block. So, the length of this phase is $1/2k$, k, $1^1/2k$, $\lfloor 1^1/2k \rfloor + 1$, and $1^1/2k + 1$ iterations, respectively.

The last block gives the remainder of $RealV$ and $RealH$ for the five cases. These moves will be played in the second phase, where we pessimistically suppose that any vertical move destroys no horizontal move, but any horizontal move destroys 1 vertical move. So Vertical is guaranteed to win if he has at least twice as many moves as Horizontal in this phase. For the $2k \times n$ boards with $n = 3, 5$, and 7 we see that Horizontal is out of moves, guaranteeing Vertical the win. (This means that the second phase of the game is skipped.) For the $2k \times 9$ board it holds that $\lceil 1^1/2k \rceil - 2 \geq 2 \times (\lceil 1/2k \rceil - 1)$, for any $k > 0$, guaranteeing Vertical the win. For the $2k \times 11$ boards, we see that Vertical has exactly twice as many moves as Horizontal, irrespective of k, enough for Vertical to win the game.

Finally, for the cases $2k \times 3$, $2k \times 7$, and $2k \times 11$ with k is odd, we note that Vertical then even has one DD move more than Horizontal, assuring him an even easier win. The proof is given by extending the first phase with one additional horizontal move, which only destroys 1 in stead of 2 vertical moves. Then the rest of the analysis is the same, with Vertical having one more move for the remainder in the second phase, giving k, k, and $2k - 1$ vertical moves for $2k \times 3$, $2k \times 7$, and $2k \times 11$ boards, respectively, all being larger than the number of horizontal moves in this phase (0, 0, and $k - 1$, respectively).   □

We note that applying this method to wider $2k \times n$ boards with odd n does not lead to additional theorems. For $n \geq 13$ the number of safe moves built by Vertical in the first phase might be not enough to oppose the number of horizontal moves. As a case in point, the 2×13 and 4×13 boards are known to be wins for Horizontal. For even wider boards of this type, vertical wins become rare, including only 2×15 and 2×19 as far as known up to date (see Appendix A).

Theorem 3. *All* $3 \times n$ *boards* $(n > 3)$ *are a win for Horizontal*

This theorem is the counterpart of Theorem 1, except that Vertical still moves first. As a consequence, a few small boards can be won by Vertical, even though Horizontal has more moves. These are the 3×2 and 3×3 boards. For boards of width at least 4, the proof is as follows.

Proof. The best case for Vertical is when n is a 4-fold + 3, since then Vertical has 1 more DD move than Horizontal + one additional column, with Vertical to move. So suppose $n = 4k + 3$. Then $RealV = 4k + 3$. Since in every pair of empty columns both Vertical and Horizontal have 1 DD move, every group of 4 columns implies 1 iteration, in which Vertical and Horizontal both play a DD move, effectively diminishing the number of real moves of both sides by 3. So after k iterations, $RealV = k + 3$. Since every DD move by Horizontal creates 2 safe moves, the total number of safe moves of Horizontal after k iterations has

Table 6. Relevant information in the proof of Theorem 4.

	$3 \times 2k$ k even	$5 \times 2k$	$7 \times 2k$ k even	$9 \times 2k$	$11 \times 2k$ k even
At start					
$RealH$	$3k$	$5k$	$7k$	$9k$	$11k$
$RealV$	$2k$	$4k$	$6k$	$8k$	$10k$
DD	k	$2k$	$3k$	$4k$	$5k$
# iter. 1st phase	$1/2k$	k	$1^1/2k$	$2k$	$2^1/2k$
After 1st phase					
$RealH$	$1^1/2k$	$2k$	$2^1/2k$	$3k$	$3^1/2k$
$RealV$	$1/2k$	k	$1^1/2k$	$2k$	$2^1/2k$
$SafeH$	k	k	$1^1/2k$	$\lfloor 1^1/2k \rfloor$	$1^1/2k$
# iter. 3rd phase	$1/2k$	k	$1^1/2k$	$\lfloor 1^1/2k \rfloor$	$1^1/2k$
Remainder for 2nd phase					
$RealH$	k	k	k	$\lceil 1^1/2k \rceil$	$2k$
$RealV$	0	0	0	$\lceil 1/2k \rceil$	k

been increased to $2k$. Since $2k \geq k + 3$ for all $k \geq 3$, it follows that Horizontal has at least as many safe moves left as all moves of Vertical for boards $3 \times n$ with $n \geq 12$. Using the fact that the boards $3 \times n$ with $4 \leq n \leq 11$ are known to be a win for Horizontal also, completes the proof that Horizontal wins all $3 \times n$ boards for $n > 3$.   □

Theorem 4. *All $m \times 2k$ boards for $m = 5$ and 9, all $m \times 2k$ boards with $k > 1$ for $m = 3$ and 7, and all $11 \times 4k$ boards are a win for Horizontal*

This theorem is the counterpart of Theorem 2. For the cases with an even number of DD moves, i.e., $5 \times 2k$ and $9 \times 2k$ for any k, and $3 \times 2k$, $7 \times 2k$, and $11 \times 2k$ for even k, the proof is similar as of Theorem 2.

Proof. We again start by giving relevant information in Table 6.

Since Horizontal is the second player, he has the advantage that he does not need the additional move in phase 3 as Vertical needs for a vertical win, as was the case in the proof of Theorem 2. On the other hand, for the cases $7 \times 2k$, $9 \times 2k$, and $11 \times 2k$ the number of safe moves guaranteed for Horizontal is one less than those for Vertical in the similar cases covered by Theorem 2.

The analysis shown in Table 6 reveals that for all three cases $3 \times 2k$ with k even, $5 \times 2k$ for any k, and $7 \times 2k$ for k even, Horizontal has k moves left to be used in phase 2, whereas Vertical has no moves left for that phase, guaranteeing a win for Horizontal. For $9 \times 2k$ for any k, Horizontal has $\lceil 1^1/2k \rceil$ moves left which for any $k > 0$ is at least twice the number of vertical moves for this phase, being $\lceil 1/2k \rceil$, again guaranteeing a horizontal win. Further, for the $11 \times 2k$ boards with k even Horizontal has $2k$ moves left for phase 2, exactly twice the number Vertical has, again assuring a horizontal win.

What remains are the three cases $3 \times 2k$, $7 \times 2k$, and $11 \times 2k$, all for odd k. Here Horizontal has the disadvantage that Vertical can make one more DD move in the first phase. For the analysis, we again prolong the first phase with one horizontal move, which however is not guaranteed to destroy any vertical move in stead of 2. Therefore, compared with the three cases with even k, Vertical has 2 additional moves left for phase 2. For $3 \times 2k$ and $7 \times 2k$, both with odd k, this means that Horizontal has k moves left for phase 2, while Vertical has 2. That means that Horizontal has at least twice the number of vertical moves and thus a guaranteed win in these cases when $k > 1$. Finally, for the $11 \times 2k$ boards with odd k Horizontal has $2k$ moves for phase 2, while Vertical has $k + 2$, thus never guaranteeing Horizontal a win.   □

The theorems agree with results in [13], reporting game-theoretical values based on translational considerations involving smaller boards for which search was needed.

7   Conclusions

In this paper we have introduced the concept of *perfect solving*, which means solving without any search. The main conclusion is that this concept can fruitfully be applied to the game of Domineering. Of the 81 non-trivial boards up to 10×10 this method was able to solve 67 perfectly. We then applied our method also to larger boards (with sizes up to 30×30) and perfectly solved 216 more boards. Most of these have not been investigated by search before, but have known game-theoretic values, based on translational considerations [13]. All our results fully agree with the known game-theoretic values.

Further, triggered by the results, we theoretically proved that all $m \times 3$ boards ($m > 1$) and all $2k \times n$ boards ($n = 3, 5, 7, 9$, and 11) are wins for Vertical. Analogously, all $3 \times n$ boards ($n > 3$), all $m \times 2k$ boards ($m = 3, 5, 7$, and 9) except 3×2 and 7×2, and all $11 \times 4k$ boards are wins for Horizontal. These results fully agree with the findings by Lachman and coworkers [13].

Finally, we believe that this paper also provides much additional insight into this intriguing game, which surely will lead to further findings (see also the next section). An update of all game-theoretic results known to date has been made available by the author [15] and will be maintained in the future.

8   Future Research

There are several directions for future research.

First, we plan to develop even more powerful rules to perfectly solve more Domineering boards. This is promising since several of the boards not solved yet have at the highest knowledge level used small deficits for the winning side. This indicates that a rule that gives a small additional reduction might be enough to solve several more boards. A first line of research is a more detailed analysis of the number of safe moves obtainable by the players. While the numbers used in the level-5 rules and level-6 rules are guaranteed, they in fact give lower bounds, but it is known that for reasonably wide or high boards the number of safe moves obtainable can be higher. This research is in progress. Further, since the knowledge rules developed so far focus on the opening and endgame of a Domineering game (only the part of the level-6 rules concerning the destroyability of 2 opponent moves after playing an xDD move concerns the middle game), we believe that new knowledge rules should concentrate on the middle game. In particular we plan to investigate rules that show in what situations in the middle game moves of the opponent are destroyable or moves of the current player are not destroyable.

Second, we are already implementing our knowledge rules into a search-based Domineering solver in order to solve more boards, especially boards that have not been solved so far. We note that implementation of the knowledge rules in a search-based solver is not straightforward, especially the higher-level ones, since determining the number of move types on an empty rectangular board is much easier than determining it for general boards encountered during search. Preliminary results (up to knowledge level 5) indicate that this approach is very effective, for most complex boards yielding orders-of-magnitude reductions compared to OBSEQUI, the best search-based solver to date. Results will be published separately in the near future.

Third, we plan to extend the theorems to cover more general cases. Whereas Theorems 1 and 2 cover cases where Vertical wins on boards with odd width up to width 11, it is clear that Vertical also will win on boards with even width or on boards with odd width larger than 11, provided that they are "vertically extended" enough. Similar expectations exist for Horizontal. It is planned to set up and prove theorems covering such cases.

Fourth, although Domineering is a combinatorial game, we so far made no use of results from combinatorial game theory. In particular, treating larger boards as disjunctive sums of smaller boards might be useful. Although we do not see how this fruitfully can be applied to perfectly solving boards, since the boards not solved so far are far too big for CGT analysis, we do expect it to be applicable during a search-based approach, especially at the end of search variations.

A   Appendix

In this appendix we provide fuller details on the results for all $m \times n$ boards for m and $n \geq 2$ and ≤ 30. We first summarize the boards solved *per level*, distinguishing them into wins for Vertical and wins for Horizontal.

Level 3

Wins for Vertical: 2×3, 6×3, 10×3, 14×3, 18×3, 22×3, 26×3, 30×3; 8 in total.
Wins for Horizontal: 3×4, 3×8, 3×12, 3×16, 3×20, 3×24, 3×28; 7 in total.

Level 4

Wins for Vertical: 2×2, 6×2, 10×2, 3×3, 4×3, 7×3, 8×3, 9×3, 11×3, 12×3, 13×3, 15×3, 16×3, 17×3, 19×3, 20×3, 21×3, 23×3, 24×3, 25×3, 27×3, 28×3, 29×3, 2×5, 4×5, 6×5, 8×5, 10×5, 12×5, 14×5, 15×5, 16×5, 17×5, 18×5, 19×5, 20×5, 21×5, 22×5, 23×5, 24×5, 25×5, 26×5, 27×5, 28×5, 29×5, 30×5, 2×7, 4×7, 6×7, 8×7, 10×7, 12×7, 14×7, 16×7, 18×7, 20×7, 22×7, 24×7, 26×7, 27×7, 28×7, 30×7, 2×11, 6×11, 10×11, 2×15, 2×19; 67 in total.

Wins for Horizontal: 5×2, 9×2, 5×4, 7×4, 9×4, 3×5, 3×6, 5×6, 9×6, 5×8, 7×8, 9×8, 3×9, 3×10, 5×10, 9×10, 3×11, 5×12, 7×12, 9×12, 3×13, 5×13, 3×14, 5×14, 7×14, 9×14, 3×15, 5×15, 5×16, 7×16, 9×16, 3×17, 5×17, 3×18, 5×18, 7×18, 9×18, 3×19, 5×19, 5×20, 7×20, 9×20, 3×21, 5×21, 3×22, 5×22, 7×22, 9×22, 3×23, 5×23, 5×24, 7×24, 9×24, 3×25, 5×25, 3×26, 5×26, 7×26, 9×26, 3×27, 5×27, 5×28, 7×28, 9×28, 3×29, 5×29, 3×30, 5×30, 7×30, 9×30; 70 in total.

Level 5

Wins for Vertical: 3×2, 7×2, 11×2, 14×2, 15×2, 18×2, 19×2, 22×2, 23×2, 26×2, 27×2, 30×2, 5×3, 11×5, 13×5, 11×7, 15×7, 17×7, 19×7, 21×7, 23×7, 25×7, 29×7, 2×9, 4×9, 6×9, 8×9, 10×9, 12×9, 14×9, 16×9, 18×9, 20×9, 22×9, 24×9, 26×9, 28×9, 30×9, 4×11, 8×11, 12×11, 14×11, 16×11, 18×11, 20×11, 22×11, 24×11, 26×11, 28×11, 30×11; 50 in total.

Wins for Horizontal: 2×4, 11×4, 7×6, 2×8, 11×8, 5×9, 7×10, 5×11, 2×12, 11×12, 7×13, 2×16, 11×16, 7×17, 7×19, 2×20, 11×20, 7×21, 7×23, 2×24, 11×24, 7×25, 7×27, 2×28, 11×28, 7×29; 26 in total.

Level 6

Wins for Vertical: 4×2, 8×2, 12×2, 16×2, 20×2, 24×2, 28×2, 4×4, 6×4, 8×4, 10×4, 12×4, 14×4, 16×4, 18×4, 20×4, 22×4, 24×4, 26×4, 28×4, 30×4, 2×6, 4×6, 6×6, 8×6, 10×6, 12×6, 14×6, 16×6, 18×6, 20×6, 22×6, 24×6, 26×6, 28×6, 30×6, 2×10; 37 in total.

Wins for Horizontal: 4×8, 6×8, 4×10, 4×12, 6×12, 4×14, 4×16, 6×16, 4×18, 4×20, 6×20, 4×22, 4×24, 6×24, 4×26, 4×28, 6×28, 4×30; 18 in total.

We next provide in Table 7 an up-to-date overview of all known game-theoretic values of Domineering boards with sizes up to 30, including information on whether they are perfectly solved, solved by search or combinatorial game theory, or by using translational symmetry rules.

Table 7. Game-theoretic values of many $m \times n$ Domineering boards, for $m, n \le 30$, Vertical moving first. V or v indicates a Vertical win, H or h a Horizontal win. An uppercase character (V or H) is used for boards solved by search or combinatorial game theory, a lowercase character (v or h) is used when the game is solved using the translational symmetry rules. An overline on any character means that our program perfectly solves the game.

$m\backslash n$	2	3	4	5	6	7	8	9	10	11	12	13	14	15	16	17	18	19	20	21	22	23	24	25	26	27	28	29	30
2	V̄	V̄	H̄	V̄	V̄	V̄	H̄	V̄	V̄	V̄	H̄	H	V	V̄	H̄	H	V	V̄	H̄	V	V̄	H̄	H	H	V	V̄	H̄	H	H
3	V̄	V̄	H̄	H̄	H̄	H̄	H̄	H̄	H̄	H̄	H̄	H̄	H̄	H̄	H̄	H̄	H̄	H̄	H̄	H̄	H̄	H̄	H̄	H̄	H̄	H̄	H̄	H̄	H̄
4	V̄	V̄	V̄	V̄	V̄	V̄	H̄	V̄	H̄	V̄	H̄	H	H̄	H	H̄	H	H̄	H̄	H	h̄	H	h̄	h	h̄	h	h̄	h	h̄	h̄
5	H̄	V̄	H̄	H	H̄	H	H̄	H	H̄	H̄	H̄	H̄	H̄	H̄	H̄	h̄	h	h̄	h	h̄	h	h̄	h	h̄	h	h̄	h	h̄	h
6	V̄	V̄	V̄	V̄	V̄	V̄	H̄	V̄	V	V̄	H̄	V	H		h̄				h̄		h		h̄		h		h̄		h
7	V̄	V̄	H̄	V̄	H̄	V̄	H̄	H̄	H	H̄	h̄	h̄	h	h̄	h	h̄	h̄	h̄	h̄	h̄	h̄	h̄	h̄	h̄	h̄	h̄	h̄	h̄	h̄
8	V̄	V̄	V̄	V̄	V̄	V̄	V̄	V̄	H	v̄		v			h				h						h				h
9	H̄	V̄	H̄	V̄	H̄	V̄	H̄	V̄	h̄		h̄		h̄		h̄		h̄		h̄			h	h̄	h	h̄	h	h̄	h	h̄
10	V̄	V̄	V̄	V̄	V̄	V̄	V̄	v̄	V	v̄		v							h										
11	V̄	V̄	H̄	V̄	V̄	V̄	h̄	v			h̄				h̄				h̄		h		h̄		h		h̄		h
12	V̄	V̄	V̄	V̄	V̄	v̄		v̄		v̄		v											h						
13	H̄	V̄	H̄	V̄	h	v	h	v	h		h		h		h		h		h		h		h						h
14	V̄	V̄	V̄	V̄	V̄	v̄		v̄		v̄		v											h						
15	V̄	V̄	V	V̄		v̄		v		v																			h
16	V̄	V̄	V̄	V̄	v̄	v̄		v̄		v̄		v																	
17	V	V̄	V		v̄		v̄		v																				
18	V̄	V̄	V̄	v̄	v̄	v̄	v	v̄		v̄		v																	
19	V̄	V̄	V	v̄	v	v̄		v		v		v																	
20	V̄	V̄	v̄	v̄	v̄	v̄	v	v̄		v̄		v																	
21	V	V̄	V		v̄			v̄		v		v																	
22	V̄	V̄	v̄	v̄	v̄	v̄		v̄	v	v̄		v																	
23	V̄	V̄	v	v̄	v	v̄		v		v		v																	
24	V̄	V̄	v̄	v̄	v̄	v̄	v	v̄		v̄		v																	
25	V	V̄	v	v̄	v	v̄		v				v																	
26	V̄	V̄	v̄	v̄	v̄	v̄	v	v̄	v	v̄		v																	
27	V̄	V̄	v	v̄	v	v̄		v		v		v																	
28	V̄	V̄	v̄	v̄	v̄	v̄	v	v̄		v̄		v																	
29	V	V̄	v	v̄		v̄		v				v																	
30	V̄	V̄	v̄	v̄	v̄	v̄	v	v̄	v	v̄		v	v																

References

1. Albert, M.H., Nowakowski, R.J., Wolfe, D.: Lessons in Play: An Introduction to Combinatorial Game Theory. A K Peters, Wellesley (2007)
2. Berlekamp, E.R.: Blockbusting and domineering. J. Combin. Theor. (Ser. A) **49**, 67–116 (1988)
3. Berlekamp, E.R., Conway, J.H., Guy, R.K.: Winning Ways for your Mathematical Plays, vols. 1–3, Academic Press, London (1982); 2nd edn., in four volumes: vol. 1 (2001), vols. 2, 3 (2003), vol. 4 (2004). A K Peters, Wellesley
4. Breuker, D.M., Uiterwijk, J.W.H.M., van den Herik, H.J.: Solving 8 × 8 Domineering. Theoret. Comput. Sci. (Math Games) **230**, 195–206 (2000)
5. Bullock, N.: Domineering: solving large combinatorial search spaces. M.Sc. thesis, University of Alberta (2002)
6. Bullock, N.: Domineering: solving large combinatorial search spaces. ICGA J. **25**, 67–84 (2002)
7. Bullock, N.: Updated game theoretic values for Domineering boards. http://webdocs.cs.ualberta.ca/~games/domineering/updated.html
8. Conway, J.H.: On Numbers and Games. Academic Press, London (1976)
9. Gardner, M.: Mathematical games. Sci. Am. **230**, 106–108 (1974)
10. van den Herik, H.J., Uiterwijk, J.W.H.M., van Rijswijck, J.: Games solved: now and in the future. Artif. Intell. **134**, 277–311 (2002)
11. Kim, Y.: New values in Domineering. Theoret. Comput. Sci. (Math Games) **156**, 263–280 (1996)
12. Knuth, D.E., Moore, R.W.: An analysis of alpha-beta pruning. Artif. Intell. **6**, 293–326 (1975)
13. Lachmann, M., Moore, C., Rapaport, I.: Who wins Domineering on rectangular boards? In: Nowakowski, R.J. (ed.) More Games of No Chance, vol. 42, pp. 307–315. Cambridge University Press, MSRI Publications, Cambridge (2002)
14. Uiterwijk, J.W.H.M., van den Herik, H.J.: The advantage of the initiative. Inf. Sci. **122**, 43–58 (2000)
15. Uiterwijk, J.W.H.M.: Updated game theoretic values for Domineering boards. https://dke.maastrichtuniversity.nl/jos.uiterwijk/?page_id=39
16. Wolfe, D.: Snakes in Domineering games. Theoret. Comput. Sci. (Math Games) **119**, 323–329 (1993)

How Relevant Are Chess Composition Conventions?

Azlan Iqbal[✉]

College of Information Technology, Universiti Tenaga Nasional,
Kampus Putrajaya, Jalan IKRAM-UNITEN, 43000 Kajang, Selangor, Malaysia
azlan@uniten.edu.my

Abstract. Composition conventions are guidelines used by human composers in composing chess problems. They are particularly significant in composition tournaments. Examples include, *not having any 'check' in the first move of the solution* and *not 'dressing up' the board with unnecessary pieces*. Conventions are often associated or even directly conflated with the overall aesthetics or beauty of a composition. Using an existing experimentally-validated computational aesthetics model for three-move mate problems, we analyzed sets of computer-generated compositions adhering to at least 2, 3 and 4 comparable conventions to test if simply conforming to *more* conventions had a positive effect on their aesthetics, as is generally believed by human composers. We found slight but statistically significant evidence that it does, but only to a point. We also analyzed human judge scores of 145 three-move mate problems composed by humans to see if they had any positive correlation with the computational aesthetic scores of those problems. We found that they did not. These seemingly conflicting findings suggest two main things. First, the right amount of adherence to composition conventions in a composition has a positive effect on its perceived aesthetics. Second, human judges either do not look at the same conventions related to aesthetics in the model used or emphasize others that have less to do with beauty as perceived by the majority of players, even though they may mistakenly consider their judgements 'beautiful' in the traditional, non-esoteric sense. Human judges may also be relying significantly on personal tastes as we found no correlation between their individual scores either.

Keywords: Chess · Composition · Conventions · Human · Judge · Beauty

1 Introduction

A chess problem or composition is a type of puzzle typically created by a human composer using a chess set. It presents potential solvers with a stipulation, e.g. *White to play and mate in 3 moves*, and is usually composed with aesthetics or beauty in mind. Compositions often adhere to many 'composition conventions' as well. Examples include: *possess a solution that is difficult rather than easy*; *contain no unnecessary moves to illustrate a theme*; *have White move first and mate Black*; *have a starting position that absolutely must be possible to achieve in a real game, however*

T. Cazenave et al. (Eds.): CGW 2013, CCIS 408, pp. 122–131, 2014.
DOI: 10.1007/978-3-319-05428-5_9, © Springer International Publishing Switzerland 2014

improbable. A more comprehensive list and supporting references are provided in Sect. 3.3.1 of [1]. Composition tournaments or 'tourneys' are at present held all over the world and attract competitors from diverse backgrounds [2].

These conventions exist and are adhered to because they are generally thought to improve the quality or beauty of a composition [1]. They are also useful as a kind of standard so that "*like is compared with like*" [3]. In Sect. 3.2 of [1], a case is made for how not all conventions are prerequisites for beauty. Even so, many composers and players tend to conflate conventions with aesthetics, i.e. a 'good' composition – one that adheres to conventions – is a more *beautiful* one. Award-winning compositions are therefore among the most *beautiful*. In this article, we put this belief to the test as it tends to lead to confusion in the world of composition and how the public understands what they produce.

A review of relevant material relating to computational aesthetics in chess can be found in Chap. 2 of [1]. Notably, Sect. 2.4 of [1] explains how modern computer chess problem composition techniques starting in the late 1980s have managed to produce compositions at varying degrees of efficiency and 'quality'. However, the issue of aesthetics and how conventions actually relate to aesthetics is not explored in detail and left largely to the purview of human experts. Included also are comparable works related to Tsume-Shogi, the Japanese equivalent to chess problems. The same chapter illustrates the many problems associated with deriving an aesthetics model from the somewhat vague methods employed by human chess problem judges alone. Our methodology for this research is presented in Sect. 2. In Sect. 3 we explain the experimental setups and results. Section 4 presents a discussion of these results. We conclude the article in Sect. 5 with a summary of the main points and some ideas for future work.

2 Methodology

In this research, we used an experimentally-validated computational aesthetics model [4] to evaluate the beauty of three-move mate problems. It has been shown to be able to evaluate and rank aesthetics or beauty in a way that correlates positively and well with *domain-competent human assessment*, i.e. not necessarily 'experts' but also people with sufficient knowledge of the domain to appreciate beauty in it. The model uses formalizations of well-known aesthetic principles and themes in chess in combination with a stochastic approach, i.e. the inclusion of some randomness. All the necessary information regarding its logic, workings and validation can be obtained by the interested reader in [4].

A computer program called CHESTHETICA, which incorporates the model, was used to automatically compose three-move mate problems [5] and evaluate their aesthetics. This was necessary in the first experiment (see Sect. 3.1) – in which we tested the idea that adherence to *more* conventions leads to increased beauty – because *human* compositions tend to contain more variations (alternative lines of play) and variety of conventions than was feasible to calculate manually for each composition. Computer-generated compositions tend to feature just one forced line and fewer, more easily identifiable conventions. The problems used in this research are therefore not of the 'enumerative' kind [6]. The composing module of the program is entirely separate from the aesthetics-evaluating one. Ideally, the latter should be usable to aid the former; however, doing so has proven to be exceedingly challenging. A useful analogy may be how the ability to *rank* beautiful pieces of art does not easily translate into the ability to *create* beautiful pieces of art.

The aesthetics model incorporated into CHESTHETICA assesses primarily 'visual appeal' (see Appendix A of [4] for examples) which is what the majority of chess players and composers with sufficient (not necessarily expert) domain knowledge understand by 'beauty' in the game. Essentially, this includes, for example, tactical maneuvers like sacrifices or combinations that achieve a clear objective such as mate. 'Depth' appeal, on the other hand, relates more toward strategic or long-term maneuvers – perhaps involving many alternative lines of play – amounting to a rather esoteric understanding of the game, furthermore specifically in relation to a particular class of chess composition, e.g. three-movers, endgame studies.

In the second experiment (see Sect. 3.2), human judge scores for human-composed problems were compared against the computer's aesthetic scores to see if there was any good, positive correlation. The underlying idea is that, aside from the slippery concept of 'originality', since human judges tend to emphasize adherence to conventions [1, 3] and consider their judgements pertaining largely to 'beauty' in the sense understood by most players and composers, we would expect that there exists such a correlation with the computer's assessments. Except, of course, in unusual circumstances where there is sufficient compensation in some other aspect of the composition that the judge finds attractive. Together, these two experiments shed some light on the role conventions play in terms of 'beauty' with regard to chess problems and whether human judges are, in fact, scoring beauty as perceived by most players or something else no less relevant to their established art form [7–10].

3   Experimental Setups and Results

3.1   Conventions and Aesthetics

For the first experiment, we had CHESTHETICA automatically compose as many three-move mate problems as possible in the time available to us using both 'random' and 'experience' approaches. The 'experience' approach was based on a database of human compositions. In short, pieces are placed at random on the board or based on the probability where they are most likely to be in a chess problem. They are then tested using a chess engine to see if a forced mate exists; see [5] for a more detailed explanation. The 'experience' approach tends to be slightly more effective at composing than the random one and the two are tested here also as an extension of previous work (ibid).

For the first set of composing 'attempts', a filter of two composition conventions was applied so that the resulting compositions would (1) *not be 'cooked'*, and (2) *have no duals in their solution*. A chess problem is said to be cooked when there is a second 'key move' (i.e. first move) not intended by the composer. A solution to a composition is said to contain a 'dual' when White has more than one valid continuation after the key move. For the second set, a filter of three composition conventions was applied so that the resulting compositions would have (1) *no 'check' in the key move*, (2) *no captures in the key move*, and (3) *no key move that restricted the enemy king's movement*. For the third set, a filter of four composition conventions was applied; namely the two conventions from the first set and the first two from the second set.

These conventions were selected because they could be determined with relative certainty and were easier to implement programmatically than others. Based on the literature surveyed (see Sect. 3.3.1 of [1]) there is no particular aesthetic distinction between them or even a strict hierarchy of importance. It is important to note that since thousands of generated compositions needed to be tested for validity, manual determination of conventions was simply not feasible and doing so would have been prone to much human error. Also, the fact that, for example, two conventions were confirmed in the first set and three in the second does not exclude the possibility that more conventions – even those other than CHESTHETICA could detect – were not present, however unlikely. What can be said with some confidence is that the first set contained *at least* two conventions, the second set contained *at least* three, and the third *at least* four.

For the first two sets, there was a total of 120,000 composing attempts run in batches of 1,000 attempts, i.e. where the computer tries to generate a composition that meets all the defined criteria of success. This took approximately 70 days using two standard desktop computers running 24 h a day. For the third set, several different computers were run simultaneously over a period of approximately 5 months in order to produce the valid compositions. As the number of conventions increases, the efficiency reduces. The composing approach consumes a lot of time primarily because there are far more 'misses' than 'hits' when a chess engine is used to determine if the particular configuration of pieces produced leads to a forced mate.

The computer program used, CHESTHETICA, is also not optimized for this particular composing task. It was designed primarily to evaluate the aesthetics of a move sequence. It is not simply a matter of having more CPU cycles at one's disposal because the approach to automatic composition incorporates many different modules (e.g. random number generation, 'intelligent' piece selection, probability computation, error-correction mechanisms, looping, mate solver) that can take time to produce something, not unlike with human composers. An analogy might be existing chess-playing engines. Simply having more processing power does not necessarily make for a better engine. The quality of the heuristics and other technologies used are also highly relevant.

Table 1 shows the results. Set 3 has no composing attempts and efficiencies listed that can be compared with the other two sets because the attempts were handled differently due to time constraints. Based on past experiments, the efficiencies for the random and experience approaches for set 3 are similar, i.e. between 0.03 to 0.05 %. Despite the slightly higher mean composing efficiencies using the 'experience' approach, they were not different to a statistically significant degree from the mean composing efficiencies of the random approach. As anticipated in [5], using conventions as a filter significantly reduces the productivity of the automatic composer.

Table 2 shows the results in terms of aesthetics. The increase of 0.067 in aesthetic value in using 3 conventions instead of 2 was minor but statistically significant; two

Table 1. Automatic composing results.

	Set 1		Set 2		Set 3	
	Random	Experience	Random	Experience	*Random*	*Experience*
Composing Attempts	30,000		30,000		-	
Conventions Adhered	2		3		*4*	
Successful Compositions	429	459	303	329	*413*	*297*
Mean Composing Efficiency	1.43%	1.53%	1.01%	1.10%	-	-
Total Compositions	888		632		*710*	

Table 2. Aesthetic scores of the computer-generated compositions.

	Set 1		Set 2		Set 3	
	Random	Experience	Random	Experience	Random	Experience
Conventions Adhered	2		3		4	
Mean Aesthetic Score	2.167	2.241	2.307	2.240	2.148	2.158
Standard Deviation	0.48	0.50	0.46	0.45	0.473	0.458
Mean Aesthetic Score	2.205		2.272		2.152	
Standard Deviation	0.49		0.45		0.47	

sample t-test assuming unequal variances: $t(1425) = -2.72$, $P < 0.01$. The decrease of 0.12 in aesthetic value in using 4 conventions instead of 3 was also minor but statistically significant; two sample t-test assuming equal variances: $t(1340) = -4.77$, $P < 0.01$. Realistically, we would not usually consider small differences in aesthetic values relevant. However, given that computer-generated compositions were used and an increase of only one convention as a basis of discrimination, we are hesitant to dismiss the findings. On a side note – in relation to an extension of previous research [5] – there was a statistically significant increase in the quality of compositions generated using the 'experience' over 'random' approach for set 1 but not for set 3. For set 2, the *decrease* was not significant.

3.2 Human Judge Ratings and Aesthetics

For the second experiment, we looked at the human judge ratings of 145 compositions by human composers. These three-movers were taken from the 'FIDE Album 2001–2003'. Unfortunately, we are unable to make these positions and their scores publicly available even though other researchers may obtain them by purchasing the album [11]. In that system, three judges score each composition on a scale of 0 to 4 and the scores are then summed. The higher the total, the better the composition is considered to be. Details pertaining to judging and selection are available at [12]. Notably, there is nothing explicitly related to aesthetics mentioned. Here is an excerpt.

"Using a scale of 0 to 4 including half-points, each judge will allocate points to the entries, in accordance with the guidelines shown in Annex 1. The whole scale should be used, but the very highest scores should not occur often. The normal score for a composition good enough for publication in a magazine but without any point of real interest is 1 or 1.5 points. A composition known by the judge to be totally anticipated will attract a score of 0. A composition believed to be unsound but not computer-testable should be given a score nonetheless, since it may turn out to be sound after all. A judge who considers a composition to be incorrect should send his claim and analysis to the director together with his score." [12]

"ANNEX 1: MEANING OF THE POINT-SCALE

4: Outstanding: **must** be in the Album
3.5
3: Very good: **ought** to be in the Album
2.5
2: Good: **could** be in the Album
1.5
1: Mediocre: **ought not** to be in the Album
0.5
0: Worthless or completely anticipated: **must not** be in the Album" [12]

A chess composition is said to be 'anticipated' when its theme has already appeared in an earlier problem without the knowledge of the later composer. The board configuration therefore does not have to be exactly the same. The 145 problems from the album were also analyzed using CHESTHETICA three times on a scale of 0 to at most 5. There is actually no hard upper limit but no three-mover has ever been found to exceed 5. Due to its stochastic element, the computational aesthetics model may deliver a slightly different score the second or third time it is used to evaluate a composition. Ideally, an average score is used if a crisp value is desired. In this case, however, it was considered more suitable that three evaluations of a composition were totaled just like the three human judge scores.

Incidentally, none of the 145 problems from the album had a score of '0' attributed by any judge so we did not have to compensate for the aesthetics model's inability to detect 'lack of originality' by filtering them out, for instance. CHESTHETICA itself is not available to the public but a version of the program that can evaluate and rank three-move problems and endgame studies in terms of aesthetics is available [13], though this version cannot compose chess problems. Table 3 shows an example of how the human judge scores and computer scores were recorded.

The actual scores themselves need not use the same scale because the Spearman or rank correlation was applied. For consistency, the computer's evaluations – in total and average – were always rounded to one decimal place to match the format of the human judge scores. Beyond that, the remaining dissimilar precision in both scales (0.1 vs. 0.5) were not arbitrarily adjusted for. We found no correlation (0.00533; two-tailed, significance level of 1 %) between the judge *total* scores for the 145

Table 3. Sample human judge and computer scores.

| | Human Judge Scores | | | |
	Judge 1	Judge 2	Judge 3	Total
Composition 1	2	2.5	3	7.5
Composition 2	3.5	4	3.5	11
	Computer Scores			
	Round 1	Round 2	Round 3	Total
Composition 1	1.679	1.699	1.639	5.0
Composition 2	1.753	1.753	1.773	5.3

compositions and computer's *total* scores for them. We tested the *mean* judge scores against the *mean* of the computer's scores and still found no correlation (-0.00523; same). In other words, there was absolutely no aesthetic relationship between the human judge scores and the computer's scores. In fact, there was no significant (Pearson) correlation between the scores of judges 1 and 2 ($r = 0.062$), judges 2 and 3 ($r = -0.036$) and judges 1 and 3 ($r = 0.115$). This suggests that even between judges there is little agreement.

4   Discussion

In the first experiment which examined the significance of using more conventions to attain greater aesthetic quality (see Sect. 3.1), we found a very small yet statistically significant increase in adhering to one more convention but only in the incremental step from 2 conventions to 3. The opposite effect was found in adhering to 4. Even though no standard distinction or hierarchy of significance is known in conventions, some are clearly more related to aesthetics than others. For instance, *avoid castling moves because it cannot be proved legal* has likely less to do with beauty than say, *no 'check' in the key move*. The five conventions used in the first experiment are probably of the type that is associated more with aesthetics and this is why the results were suggestive of their contribution to beauty.

Human judges, on the other hand, do not usually standardize which conventions they should look for. Assuming they are as objective as humanly possible, they will evaluate or rate compositions by looking at both conventions that are associated with beauty and those that are less so. Not to mention factors that have little to do with anything other judges might consider relevant. Human judges also consider other intangible concepts such as 'originality' and cannot completely ignore their personal tastes. This might explain why, in the second experiment (see Sect. 3.2), we found no correlation between the human judge scores and the computer's. The issue is when the scores or rankings given by these judges are said to be based on "beauty". Beauty, as perceived by the majority of chess players and composers, is unlikely what these judges are mainly evaluating. This is not to say that human judges have no right to use the word 'beauty' but this research would suggest that that sort of beauty is actually a

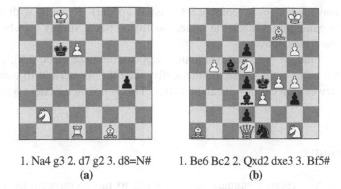

1. Na4 g3 2. d7 g2 3. d8=N#   1. Be6 Bc2 2. Qxd2 dxe3 3. Bf5#
      (a)   **(b)**

Fig. 1. The highest-scoring computer composition (a) and judge-rated problem (b).

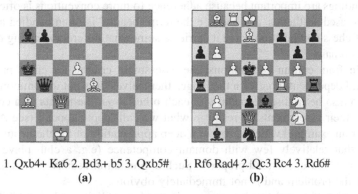

1. Qxb4+ Ka6 2. Bd3+ b5 3. Qxb5#   1. Rf6 Rad4 2. Qc3 Rc4 3. Rd6#
      (a)   **(b)**

Fig. 2. The lowest-scoring computer composition (a) and judge-rated problem (b).

combination of other things, including personal taste, that is less likely to be understood by the public.

Despite that, the evaluations of these judges are no less viable than they were before because it simply means that 'winning' compositions are not necessarily the most *beautiful*, as the term is commonly understood. There are special things about award-winning compositions that few others outside the domain of expert composition would fully understand, but 'beauty' or aesthetics as evaluated by the model plays only a small part in it. Figures 1 and 2 show the highest-scoring and lowest-scoring three-movers, respectively, from the collection of computer-generated compositions used in the first experiment and the collection of 145 compositions by human composers used in the second experiment. Only the main lines are shown.

Readers with sufficient knowledge of chess should be able to form an opinion as to how much human judges are factoring in what we understand by 'beauty' in the game. Notably, beauty in the judge-rated problems appears to be more complicated and understood properly by relatively few (depth appeal) whereas beauty in the computer-generated compositions appears to be more easily perceived and understood by the majority of players and even composers (visual appeal). Readers with no understanding of the game might reach the same conclusion based simply on what they can see from the positions above.

As for the 'random' versus 'experience' approaches (see Sect. 3.1), the results suggest that the latter is no worse, aesthetically, than the former but in compositions filtered using fewer conventions, it can be better. This is not inconsistent with previous findings [5].

5 Conclusions

The results of this research suggest that adhering to more conventions, to a point, increases the perceived aesthetic value of a chess problem and that human judges are probably not factoring this sort of (visual) beauty into their rankings or assessments. These findings are important because adherence to more conventions is often confused with increased aesthetics, and because the term 'beauty' is often bandied about in the world of chess composition when it carries a somewhat different meaning outside that esoteric domain.

Aside from certain conventions, the assessment criteria for chess problems are vague and dependent largely on the judges themselves. It is not uncommon for human judges to also be in disagreement with each other about the merits of a composition. Even so, their assessments do result in what we call 'depth appeal' (see Appendix A of [4] for an example) which is sort of a deep appreciation of the theme and variations of play that relatively few with domain competence (e.g. a club player or casual composer) could understand properly. Such appreciation usually occurs after careful study of the problem and is not immediately obvious.

If the aim of experienced composers is greater publicity and accessibility to their art form [3], then more emphasis on 'visual appeal' would be prudent in tourneys and published compositions. However, if this is considered unsuitable, then at least a clarification of what they are really looking at when evaluating chess problems would be wise as the term 'beauty' can be quite misleading, especially outside specialized composing circles. Figures 1 and 2 above perhaps illustrate the contrast between what the majority of chess players and casual composers understand by 'beauty' and what judges of tourneys do.

Further work in this area may involve examining the use of even more conventions to see if the downtrend continues or improves beyond the use of just 3. Experimentation in this regard is likely to be more difficult because automatic chess problem composition will require an exponentially longer amount of time. Human judge evaluations of other types of compositions (e.g. endgame studies) can be examined as well to see if there is any correlation with aesthetics based on the model used.

Acknowledgement. This research is sponsored in part by the Ministry of Science, Technology and Innovation (MOSTI) in Malaysia under their eScienceFund research grant (01-02-03-SF0240).

References

1. Iqbal, M.A.M.: A discrete computational aesthetics model for a zero-sum perfect information game. Ph.D. Thesis, Faculty of Computer Science and Information Technology, University of Malaya, Kuala Lumpur, Malaysia. http://metalab.uniten.edu. my/~azlan/Research/pdfs/phd_thesis_azlan.pdf (2008)
2. Giddins, S.: Problems, problems, problems. ChessBase News, 16 April 2010. http://www. chessbase.com/newsdetail.asp?newsid=6261 (2010)
3. Albrecht, H.: How should the role of a (chess) tourney judge be interpreted? The Problemist, July, 217–218 (1993). Originally published as Über Die Auffassung Des Richteramtes In Problemturnieren, Problem, January, 107–109 (1959)
4. Iqbal, A., van der Heijden, H., Guid, M., Makhmali, A.: Evaluating the aesthetics of endgame studies: a computational model of human aesthetic perception. IEEE Trans. Comput. Intell. AI in Games: Special Issue on Computational Aesthetics in Games 4(3), 178–191 (2012)
5. Iqbal, A.: Increasing efficiency and quality in the automatic composition of three-move mate problems. In: Anacleto, J.C., Fels, S., Graham, N., Kapralos, B., Saif El-Nasr, M., Stanley, K. (eds.) ICEC 2011. LNCS, vol. 6972, pp. 186–197. Springer, Heidelberg (2011)
6. Elkies, N.D.: New directions in enumerative chess problems. Electron. J. Combin. 11(2), 1–14 (2005)
7. Osborne, H.: Notes on the aesthetics of chess and the concept of intellectual beauty. Br. J. Aesthet. 4, 160–163 (1964)
8. Humble, P.N.: Chess as an art form. Br. J. Aesthet. 33, 59–66 (1993)
9. Troyer, J.G.: Truth and beauty: the aesthetics of chess problems. In: Haller (ed.) Aesthetics, pp. 126–130. Holder-Pichler-Tempsky, Vienna (1983)
10. Walls, B.P.: Beautiful mates: applying principles of beauty to computer chess heuristics. Dissertation.com, 1st edn. (1997)
11. Fougiaxis, H., Harkola, H.: World Federation for Chess Composition, FIDE Albums. http://www.saunalahti.fi/~stniekat/pccc/fa.htm, June 2013
12. Fougiaxis, H., Harkola, H.: FIDE Album Instructions. http://www.saunalahti.fi/~stniekat/pccc/fainstr.htm, January 2013
13. Iqbal, A., van der Heijden, H., Guid, M., Makhmali, A.: A computer program to identify beauty in problems and studies (What makes problems and studies beautiful? A computer program takes a look). ChessBase News, Hamburg, Germany. http://en.chessbase.com/home/TabId/211/PostId/4008602, 15 December 2012

Author Index

Bouzy, Bruno 1

Cazenave, Tristan 71

Döbbelin, Robert 16

Iqbal, Azlan 122

Kroon, Steve 44

Lanctot, Marc 28
Lisý, Viliam 28

Reinefeld, Alexander 16
Roschke, Max 57

Sato, Yuichiro 71
Schütt, Thorsten 16
Sturtevant, Nathan R. 57

Uiterwijk, Jos W.H.M. 97

Valla, Tomáš 81
van Niekerk, Francois 44
Veselý, Pavel 81

Winands, Mark H.M. 28